CW01262324

Luminous Essence

Luminous Essence

— •❖• —

A GUIDE TO THE GUHYAGARBHA TANTRA

by Jamgön Mipham

FOREWORD BY
His Holiness the Dalai Lama

TRANSLATED BY THE
Dharmachakra Translation Committee

SNOW LION
BOSTON & LONDON

Snow Lion
An imprint of Shambhala Publications, Inc.
Horticultural Hall
300 Massachusetts Avenue
Boston, Massachusetts 02115
www.shambhala.com

© 2009 by Dharmachakra Translation Committee
Visual outline on pp. 177–179 © 2009 by Tsadra Foundation. Designed by Rafael Ortet.

All rights reserved. No part of this book may be reproduced in any form or by any means, electronic or mechanical, including photocopying, recording, or by any information storage and retrieval system, without permission in writing from the publisher.

9 8 7 6 5 4 3 2

Printed in the United States of America
♾ This edition is printed on acid-free paper that meets the American National Standards Institute Z39.48 Standard.
♻ Shambhala Publications makes every effort to print on recycled paper. For more information please visit www.shambhala.com.
Distributed in the United States by Random House, Inc., and in Canada by Random House of Canada Ltd

Designed and typeset by Gopa & Ted2, Inc.

Library of Congress Cataloging-in-Publication Data
Mi-pham-rgya-mtsho, 'Jam-mgon 'Ju, 1846–1912.
[Gsaṅ 'grel phyogs bcu'i mun sel gyi spyi don 'od gsal sñin po. English]
Luminous essence: a guide to the Guhyagarbha Tantra / by Jamgön Mipham; foreword by His Holiness the Dalai Lama; translated by the Dharmachakra Translation Committee.
p. cm.
Translated from Tibetan.
ISBN 978-1-55939-327-0 (alk. paper)
1. Tripiṭaka. Sūtrapiṭaka. Tantra. Guhyagarbhatantra—Criticism, interpretation, etc. I. Dharmachakra Translation Committee. II. Title.
BQ2180.G937 M57513 2009
294.3'85—dc22
2008054161

Table of Contents

Foreword by His Holiness the Dalai Lama	vii
Introduction by Chökyi Nyima Rinpoche	ix
Translators' Introduction	xi

Luminous Essence — 1

1) The Magnificence of the Tantra	2
2) The Meaning of the Tantra	5
1) The Title	6
2) A Summary of the Essential Points of the Meaning of the Text's Subject Matter	7
1) The Purpose and Relevance of the Tantra	7
2) Presenting the Meaning of the Tantra	9
(1) The Setting	9
(2) The Prelude	11
(3) The Meaning of the Tantra	12
(1) A General Presentation of the Principles of the Three Continua	12
(1) The Ground Continuum	12
1. The Natural Maṇḍala of the Ground	12
2. How Delusion Arises	13
3. Delusion and the Natural Ground	14
4. The Reversal of Delusion	15
(2) The Path Continuum	16
1. The Essence of the Path	16
2. The Divisions of the Path	17
1. A General Explanation	17
1. The Two Vehicles	17

2. The Five Vehicles	17
3. The Nine Vehicles	23
2. The Path of Unsurpassable Mantra	24
1. Development and Completion	24
2. Means and Liberation	27
3. Traversing the Path	29
(3) The Fruition Continuum	35
(2) Specific Explanation of the Path Continuum	37
(1) Various Classification Schemes	37
(2) The Present Context	38
1. View	38
2. Absorption	68
3. Conduct	77
4. Maṇḍala	84
5. Empowerment	88
6. Samayas	93
7. Accomplishment	112
8. Offerings	123
9. Enlightened Activity	130
10. Mudrā	138
11. Mantra	144
(4) Conclusion: The Full and Complete Entrustment	159
(1) Entrusting the Profound Meaning of the Tantra in a Nondual Manner	159
(2) The Superiority of the Recipients to Whom This Tantra Is Entrusted	162
3) Extensive Explanation of the Meaning Expressed through the Words of the Tantra	165

Appendices

Appendix A: Topical Outline of *Luminous Essence*	169
Appendix B: Expanded Outline of the Topic "The Present Context" from the Topical Outline of *Luminous Essence*	171
Appendix C: Visual Outline of *Luminous Essence*	175

·⁂· Foreword ·⁂·

READING IS IMPORTANT to me, and I am often reminded of the great kindness of the scholars and translators of the past who translated a vast array of Buddhist literature into Tibetan. Through their persistent efforts, working in small teams, they made books available to Tibetans that allowed a deep understanding of the Buddha's teachings to take root in Tibet. It was this understanding that later found expression in the many books composed by Tibetan authors. Therefore, it gives me great pleasure to know that there are groups of experienced translators today, similar to those of the past, such as the Dharmachakra Translation Committee, who are working steadily to translate Buddhist books from Tibetan into English and other Western languages. Undoubtedly these will make an invaluable contribution to a deep and lasting understanding of the Buddhist tradition.

One of the most accomplished scholars and prolific writers of recent times in Tibet was Jamgön Mipham Rinpoche. An eclectic master, who was prominent in the nonsectarian movement that flourished, particularly in Eastern Tibet, in the late nineteenth and early twentieth centuries, his works are regarded as authoritative.

I am pleased to know that great care has been taken in preparing this translation of *Luminous Essence*, Mipham Rinpoche's commentary on the *Guhyagarbha Tantra*, the root tantra which reveals mind and wisdom to be naturally manifest. It is inspiring to know that the project has received the blessing and guidance of such eminent contemporary masters as Kyabje Dilgo Khyentse Rinpoche and Trulshik Rinpoche, who have also showed great kindness as teachers to me.

I have no doubt that interested and initiated practitioners of the *Guhyagarbha Tantra* cycle of practices will derive great benefit from reading and relying on this explanatory text. I congratulate all who have participated in this work of translation and offer my prayers that the good you have done will make a far-reaching contribution to peace and enlightenment in the world.

His Holiness the Dalai Lama

·:· Introduction ·:·

I AM PLEASED to present the community of tantric practitioners with this translation of Jamgön Mipham Rinpoche's *Luminous Essence*. Mipham Rinpoche's eloquent and profound treatise is a general commentary on the meaning of the famed *Tantra of the Secret Essence*, the *Guhyagarbha-tantra*, which reveals mind and wisdom to be self-display. When studying a profound text such as this, it is imperative to proceed in an authentic manner with the blessing of the lineage. In the case of the tantric scriptures, this means to receive the appropriate empowerments, reading transmissions, and oral explanations of the text from a qualified lineage master. Simply reading the text on one's own will not facilitate a genuine understanding of either the words or their meaning.

For this reason, it is crucial to first seek out a genuine master of the lineage who possesses both experience and realization based on the view of inseparable purity and equality. From such a master one must receive the ripening empowerments, the supportive reading transmission, and the liberating oral instructions. Finally, having received the complete transmission of the text, one must be diligent in putting it into practice and so liberate oneself into the fruition of the Great Perfection.

In order to serve the community of practitioners, the Dharmachakra Translation Committee has now prepared an English translation of Mipham Rinpoche's *Luminous Essence*, which lays out the fundamental framework for tantric theory and practice. The encouragement to propagate this text I received in particular from Kyabje Dudjom Rinpoche and Kyabje Dilgo Khyentse Rinpoche. The translation has been produced with the kind help of several accomplished teachers, headed by Kyabje Trulshik Rinpoche, who most kindly conferred the empowerments for the *Tantra of the Secret Essence* upon the team of translators.

May all merit in producing this text become the cause of happiness and awakening for all beings.

Chökyi Nyima Rinpoche
President, Dharmachakra Translation Committee

❖ Translators' Introduction ❖

THE PRESENT TRANSLATION of Jamgön Mipham Rinpoche's *Luminous Essence* has been produced as a group project involving several translators who based their efforts on the oral instructions of several expert teachers. In particular, the translation relied on the explanations of Khenpo Sherab Sangpo, who taught the complete text at Ka-Nying Shedrub Ling Monastery in Boudhanath during the summer months of 2005. In addition, the translation benefited greatly from the additional teachings of Khenpo Sherab Dorje, Khenpo Tsültrim Lodrö, Khenpo Kātyāyana, and Tulku Nyima Gyeltsen. For the translation of the root verses of the *Tantra of the Secret Essence*, the translation primarily relies on Longchenpa's famed commentary in his *Dispelling the Darkness of the Ten Directions,* as well as Khenpo Shenga's interlinear commentary. The translation was produced by Thomas Doctor, Heidi Köppl, Douglas Duckworth, Andreas Doctor, and Cortland Dahl. The various translations were compiled and checked against the original Tibetan by Andreas Doctor before finally being edited by Cortland Dahl.

Traditionally, tantric teachings such as these have been kept secret from the general public since the profound nature of their contents makes them likely to be misunderstood. However, based on the personal advice and public statements made by several senior masters, it appears that the benefit of keeping tantric teachings secret is now outweighed by the danger of not making genuine teachings available in a time when tantric teachings of dubious origin proliferate in print and on the internet. This view is also one that His Holiness the Dalai Lama has expressed on several occasions. For example, in his introduction to *Tantra in Tibet* (1987, Snow Lion Publications) His Holiness says: "In general, translating a book of Mantra for sale in shops is unsuitable, but at this time and in this situation there is greater fault in not clearing away wrong ideas than there is in distributing translations. Much falsely ascribed information about Secret Mantra has wide repute nowadays, and therefore, I think that translating and distributing authoritative books may help to clear away false superimpositions."

It is with this advice in mind that the present translation is now being published by Snow Lion Publications. However, the fact that the translation is being distributed publically should not lessen the importance of the advice given by all traditional authorities on tantric thought and practice: to fully understand the message contained in the profound tantric scriptures, it is essential to receive the appropriate empowerments, reading transmissions, and oral instructions before finally putting the teaching into practice through meditation. To reflect the necessity of relying on a living master to clear away questions and doubts regarding the topics discussed in texts such as this, we have presented the translation without an introductory discourse or any form of annotation. It is hoped that this will prompt the reader to seek out a genuine master who can transmit the teaching in its entirety so that the great tantric wisdom traditions of India and Tibet may gain a solid footing as they spread to new regions of the world.

The translators wish to express their profound gratitude to Chökyi Nyima Rinpoche and all other learned and accomplished teachers, who with wisdom and compassion guided our feeble efforts to convey the beauty and profundity of Lama Mipham's sacred words into English. We also wish to humbly convey our thanks to His Holiness the Dalai Lama for blessing this publication in his foreword. The entire translation process has enjoyed the kind support of the Tsadra Foundation in the form of a generous grant for which we are most thankful. We also wish to thank Snow Lion Publications for publishing this text and for their efforts in bringing Buddhism to the Western world.

We sincerely regret and apologize for any errors and mistakes this translation may contain. They are exclusively ours, caused by our superficial understanding of the profound nature of Mantra. Whatever goodness may come from the translation, we dedicate it to the benefit and happiness of all sentient beings.

On behalf of the team of translators,
Andreas Doctor

सर्वतन्त्रस्य दशदिग्बन्धकारस्य गीतानाम् सामान्यार्थं विदधतिस्म ।

❖ Luminous Essence ❖

An Overview of the Commentary on the *Secret Essence* Entitled
Dispelling the Darkness of the Ten Directions

Namo gurumañjughoṣāya!

The radiance of spontaneously present awareness,
Inseparable from the inner basic space of primordial purity and simplicity,
The wisdom body, free from aging and decay –
Youthful Mañjuśrī, please bestow auspiciousness!

Within the basic space of the ground, the equality of all phenomena,
You have perfected the strength of reveling in the self-manifest three bodies—
Immaculate and primordial protector Longchenpa,
Drime Özer, give me strength!

Lion of Speech, the fire of your reasoning
Scorched the entire thicket of mistaken teachings in this world.
You who discovered the gentle and glorious body of nectar,
Rongzom Chökyi Sangpo, may you be victorious!

Masters and knowledge holders of the mind, symbolic and oral transmissions,

Yidam deities assuming appearances of peace, passion and wrath,
Ḍākinīs of the three places, and hosts of the three classes of haughty
 spirits—
Infinite deities of the three roots, homage and veneration to you!

The lion's roar of the supreme vehicle—
Appearance and existence primordially the great bliss of purity
 and equality—
Terrifies the herds of deer that teach falsely throughout the three worlds.
The vital points in the meaning of the profound and vast vajra tantras,

Of the early translations of secret mantra, with their six-fold greatness,
I shall here explain in a concise overview of the essence,
An excellent teaching that vanquishes the darkness of the ten directions,
With the expansive light of the sun and moon.

The *Great Tantra of the Glorious Magical Net, the Secret Essence, Reality Ascertained* reveals mind and wisdom to be self-display. The explanation of this tantra contains two sections: (1) the magnificence of the tantra that is being taught and (2) an explanation of its meaning.

1. THE MAGNIFICENCE OF THE TANTRA

This universal tantra of the great *Magical Net* is a secret among secrets. It clarifies the key points of the intent of the ocean-like mantra tantras of the vajra vehicle. In a general statement, the *Tantra of the Heart Mirror of Vajrasattva* declares:

> The development of mahāyoga is like the ground of all doctrines.
> The completion of anuyoga is like the path of all doctrines.
> The great perfection of atiyoga is like the fruition of all doctrines.

Accordingly, mahāyoga teaches the complete nature of the ground, path, and fruition of the entire mantra vehicle. It is, therefore, essential to develop certainty regarding all aspects of mantra practice based on mahāyoga. Mahāyoga belongs to the inner tantras of secret mantra, and can itself be divided into an infinite number of categories. These all come about through the play of wisdom of the magical net. The latter, moreover, possesses an infinite number of practices related to deity, mantra, and meditative absorption, each of which is designed to suit the constitutions, capacities, and wishes of those in need of training. For this reason, it is impossible to fathom the full extent of these practices. From the perspective of their essence, however, they can be divided into two categories: (1) the vast tantras of the common variety and (2) the profound tantras of the extraordinary essence.

As for the former, all the infinite categories of tantra can, generally speaking, be included in six classes of tantra: the five classes of enlightened body, speech, mind, qualities, and activity, plus their indivisibility, the class of the universal master heruka, also known as the class of the sixth, the vajra holder. In terms of what they express, these tantras can also be divided into those that primarily teach the aspect of means, those that primarily teach the aspect of knowledge, and those that emphasize the wisdom of nondual means and knowledge. Respectively, these three approaches are the father, mother, and nondual tantras. These three classes are exemplified by the *Gathering of Secrets*, which clearly teaches the illusory body; the *Wheel of Supreme Bliss*, which primarily teaches luminosity; and the *Wheel of Time*, which emphasizes the wisdom of unity. Because the *Wheel of Time* emphasizes that which is to be revealed, the ultimate wisdom of unity itself, it is known as "the androgynous stage of Vajrasattva." In this way, it is classified as a nondual tantra. This is also the reasoning behind the subdivisions of the Nyingma School's mantra scriptures, such as the classification of mahāyoga into three parts, starting with the mahā of mahā.

Secondly, the profound and extraordinary tantras are divided into the vast Tantra Section and the profound Sādhana Section. The Tantra Section consists of the renowned "Eighteen Great Tantras." The basis or essence of all of these is the *Tantra of the Secret Essence*. Why are these tantras extraordinary and profound? It is because these tantras are the avenue whereby one may arrive at the unmistaken realization of the central points of the intent of all the inner tantra sections of secret mantra. The entirety of the unsurpassable mantra is alike in that one is first ripened by the four empowerments and then applies the key points of the path of the two stages. Nevertheless, most other tantras tend to teach the practices of deity and mantra alone, as well as the methods for applying the key points concerning the channels, energies, and essences in the completion stage. Moreover, all of these key points are subsumed in the view of the great purity and equality of appearance and existence, and in the explicit introduction to the ultimate wisdom that is to be revealed. While this remains concealed in vajra statements elsewhere, in these tantras it is taught explicitly. In the *Wheel of Time*, for example, the key points hidden by the Vajra Possessor within vajra statements are taught clearly. For this reason, that tantra is known as "the open jewel casket of the buddhas."

Also, while the wisdom of the fourth empowerment is the core of the path of the vajra vehicle, other tantras describe it with statements such as, "the fourth is also like that." Thus, they do not teach it explicitly, but simply leave it as something to be induced by the third empowerment. Because of this, many Indians who taught the key points of the tantras identified the wisdom of the fourth empowerment merely as the blissful sensation of union, the mind free from attachment, or the intellectual understanding of emptiness, and so forth. These notions have been clearly refuted in certain treatises, such as the commentary on the *Sevenfold Union* and Indrabhūti's *Accomplishment of Wisdom*.

These days, there is abundant delusion here in the Cool Abode as well. For example, there are some who denigrate the pith instructions that point out the wisdom of the fourth empowerment, who assert the recent convergence of a blissful feeling and the notion of emptiness to be the co-emergent, and so forth. Considering all this, one must apply the teachings of the *Wheel of Time* universally when approaching the key points of the collected tantras. This is a genuine pith instruction. The elucidations of the *Wheel of Time* and its commentary, the *Accomplishment of Wisdom*, are of exceptional clarity. They deal with topics such as the nondual wisdom-body of immutable bliss and emptiness endowed with all supreme aspects, the ultimate co-emergent to be revealed, and the sky-like Vajra Possessor beyond the phenomena of matter and mind, yet pervading all of space.

It is said that tantras must be understood based on other tantras, and this great *Tantra of the Secret Essence* reveals all the key points concerning the view and meditation of the unsurpassable mantra; nothing is kept hidden. It also establishes the intended meaning of the entire vajra vehicle. For this reason, it is the single jewel of the three worlds, the king of all tantras, the pinnacle of all vehicles, the source of all teachings, the universal explanation of all scripture, the great highway of all the buddhas, and the sacred heart of the intent of all thus-gone ones. Its magnificent qualities are amazing.

However, lacking the essential points as taught in this tantra, treatises are composed recklessly with a limited understanding of a few profound vajra statements in the mantra tantras. In accordance with peoples' individual mental capacities, they are treated as conceptual issues meant for logicians. Knowing such texts to be devoid of the essential points, like a dead, lifeless corpse, fortunate individuals with a supreme aspiration toward the vajra vehicle will do well in wholeheartedly pursuing the study and teaching of a tantra such as this, doing so without concern for their own body or life.

2. THE MEANING OF THE TANTRA

Regarding the explanation of the tantra's meaning, there are two great chariot traditions: (1) the vast, common explanatory tradition and (2) the profound, uncommon explanatory tradition. The first is the wondrous approach of the glorious Zur, the king of all knowledge mantra holders, which explains the tantra according to mahāyoga's own scriptural tradition. The second represents the unsurpassable intent of the two lions of speech, Rongzom and Longchenpa.

The *Tantra of the Secret Essence* is the ati of mahā, which is the same as the mahā of ati in terms of the three divisions of the great perfection. In this way, the secret great perfection can be explained in three ways: (1) by revealing indivisible development and completion as the self-displayed maṇḍala of mind and wisdom; (2) through pointing out how mind in essence is the nature of primordial enlightenment, independent of development and completion; and (3) by showing that wisdom is the nature of enlightenment as the essence of self-display. Here the explanation will be given in terms of the first of these three.

While the aforementioned two explanatory traditions are of the same taste concerning their realization of the final key points, the explanation given here will follow the latter tradition, which possesses the essential points of profound pith instructions. There are three parts to this explanation: (1) an explanation of the meaning of the text's title, which is one way to realize its subject matter; (2) an explanation that summarizes the essential points of the meaning of this subject matter; and (3) an extensive explanation of the meaning expressed through the words of the tantra.

1. The Title

A title engenders understanding in those of the sharpest faculties, just as the word "vase" elicits an awareness of a bulbous object. Thus, in realizing the meaning of its title, such individuals will also comprehend the meaning of the tantra itself, which teaches how all phenomena are primordially the maṇḍala of buddhahood. Let us begin, therefore, by explaining the meaning of the title.

Generally, the Sanskrit word "tantra" is translated as "continuum." In this way, tantra refers to the continued presence of statements and meanings that reveal the relationship between deities, mantras, and meditative absorption, the various means for actualizing the supreme and common accomplishments that are sought after. In particular, the *Secret Essence—Reality Ascertained* can be explained as follows. All phenomena of saṃsāra and nirvāṇa are inseparable with the enlightened state; they dwell primordially as the eternal wheel of adornment of enlightened body, speech, and mind. This is what is meant by the term *secret*. It is referred to as such because those who are obscured and unfit to receive these teachings do not realize this, although it is genuinely realized by the profound wisdom mind of the victorious ones. It is secret in the sense that the three bodies go unrecognized due to the veils of temporary obscurations, though they are present within. Moreover, the profound views that reveal this presence are not known through one's own power, nor are they pointed out by another, and, even if they are, they are hard to realize. In this way, they are hidden. Furthermore, unless this special view, meditation, and conduct are concealed from those who are unfit to receive these teachings, the seal of secrecy will be broken and they will be misconstrued. Therefore, it is not taught to such individuals and must be concealed. In this way, it is secret, both in the sense of being unseen and concealed.

The term *essence* refers to the final, actual way of all phenomena—primordial enlightenment as the embodiment of the eternal wheel of adornment of enlightened body, speech, and mind. This is the equality of the great perfection, along with the profound and vast expressions of that state. It is referred to as the essence because it is the ground, the extract, and the quintessence of all phenomena.

The term *reality* refers to the very nature of the three bodies, which are beyond meeting and parting. This nature pervades all entities and is the sole identity of everything. It is the reality of the natural state. It is unmistaken and, hence, undeceiving. These words also indicate that this natural condition always remains just as it is, without any degeneration or change.

The term *ascertained* implies that the meaning of this teaching is not an expedient one meant for new students. Rather, it is the final meaning; it is revealed to fortunate disciples exactly as it is, just as it has dawned in the minds of the thus-gone ones themselves. Hence, this word shows that this is the definitive, or final, meaning.

In this way, it should be understood that these four components of the title all illustrate the meaning of the purity and equality of primordial enlightenment. They are all various perspectives on its qualities. Alternatively, one may also say that the primordial buddhahood of all phenomena is the ground, the *secret essence*. The experiential integration of that through the indivisible development and completion stages is the path, *reality*. The culmination of the path is the spontaneous presence of the three bodies. This is the fruition, *ascertained* within the ground.

One may also consider the four components of the title in a general manner, in terms of what these words refer to. From this perspective, the meaning they express concerns the ground, path, and fruition. The expressions used to communicate this meaning consist of the appearance of verbal language and audible language, with the former functioning as the cause of the latter. This also includes the symbolic representations of these sounds that are contained in books. All of the words in the title are explicable to the same extent as they are applicable. The explanation and application of their words are applied in equal measure to all of the terms in the title.

2. A Summary of the Essential Points of the Meaning of the Text's Subject Matter

This section includes: (1) an explanation of the tantra's purpose and relevance, which are points of access for wise individuals, and (2) the presentation of the meaning of the tantra that has this purpose.

1. The Purpose and Relevance of the Tantra

Those who are skilled in discerning between what to do and what to avoid may wonder, "What is the subject matter of this tantra? How is it articulated? What is the purpose of understanding this subject matter?"

In response, those who can discern the relevance of this meaning should be taught the following:

The *subject matter* of this tantra is the maṇḍala of the ground, the ultimate natural state of all phenomena, which is primordially of an enlightened nature within great purity and equality. Moreover, the tantra also shows the path, the various means that allow one to actualize this ground either directly or indirectly. Finally, the tantra reveals the maṇḍala of the fruition—perfect, total purity. In short, the tantra teaches the profound realization of mantra, as subsumed within ground, path, and fruition.

The *text* consists of the various words, sentences, and syllables that make up the twenty-two chapters of the root tantra and fully reveal their significance. Their identity is inseparable from the enlightened body, speech, and mind of all the thus-gone ones. They are the self-displayed play of the lord of the maṇḍala's wisdom, arising in the form of secret vajra statements. In the self-displayed Unexcelled Realm, they are spoken effortlessly by way of awareness and convey the meaning of self-displayed wisdom to a retinue that is not different from the teacher himself.

The tantra is also taught in the mere perception of others through the power of the buddhas' blessings and the disciples' virtue. As the final, definitive meaning, not an expedient method, it then serves to establish others in noble wisdom. Thus, when the words of this tantra of the supreme secret appear to the mind as general expressions, it is "the tantra which appears as language." Correspondingly, as one gives rise to a wish to speak, the breath is stirred. Then, the conditioning factors of the locations and instruments of language can be employed, resulting in speech. This is "the tantra of audible language." The supports or symbols for its expression are the external appearance of the syllables that are entered in books. This, then, is "the tantra in the form of symbols."

The *continuum* refers to the subject matter, the setting and so forth, being connected in terms of cause, condition, and effect, as well as this meaning being perfectly elucidated through its intimate connection with the stream of names, words, and letters of the text.

The *purpose* of the tantra is to facilitate the comprehension of the natures of the three actual continua that are represented by the continuum of syllables used in communication. When, as the mingling of word and meaning, an object universal occurs as an object to the mind, it is conceived of as if it were the specifically characterized. In this way, the symbol is joined with its referent and a convention is established. This is the case with all words.

The *essential purpose* of the tantra is to actualize the supreme and common accomplishments by realizing the meaning of its subject matter. This essential purpose depends upon the purpose, while the purpose depends upon realizing the subject matter, and realizing this meaning depends upon the words themselves. Therefore, the subject matter and the words are that which is to be known and the means for knowing it, respectively. Likewise, the words and the purpose are the method and its result, respectively. The purpose and the essential purpose stand in a causal relationship. Finally, the essential purpose and the subject matter are in a relationship of single identity.

Therefore, it should be understood that this tantra serves the purpose of easily and painlessly accomplishing both temporary and ultimate objectives. Even if one does not realize its meaning, simply hearing the sound of the tantra, or seeing a volume of the tantra, is supremely beneficial. As explained in the scriptures, such encounters are due to the power of extraordinary accumulations gathered in the past.

2. *Presenting the Meaning of the Tantra*

This section discusses: (1) the setting, which is the cause for the tantra's appearance, (2) the prelude, which is the condition, (3) the meaning of the tantra that must be fully understood, which is the fruition, and (4) the full and complete entrustment, which is the conclusion. Thus, there are four topics, equal in number to the four vajras.

1. THE SETTING

The setting concerns the five perfections. In the context of this great tantra, these five are explained in a special manner: The *teacher* is glorious Samantabhadra, the lord of the vajra body, speech, and mind of all thus-gone ones in the ten directions and four times. This teacher is taught to be complete enlightenment, the primordial nature of all phenomena. Therefore, this is unlike a teacher that is held to be a limited form body that is part of a continuum of enlightened wisdom that appears once an individual has trained on the path.

The *location* is the Unexcelled Realm, which is devoid of both center and limits. This vast and unconfined self-display is the palace of the basic space of phenomena and the maṇḍala of the essential enlightenment of all phenomena. It is not a confined realm that is located among pure and impure fields.

The *retinue* is held to consist of self-displayed emanations of great wisdom. As such, their stream of being is not different from the teacher himself, who upholds the principle of great awakening in which all defiled and undefiled phenomena are indivisible in nature. Thus, the retinue does not consist of other beings assembled through purity or faith.

The *time* is the changeless state of basic space, the equality of the four times. This eternal wheel of adornment of enlightened body, speech, and mind is effortlessly and spontaneously present as the richly arrayed ornament. It is, therefore, not a limited period divided into past, present, or future, nor is it composed of instants, moments, or otherwise.

The *tantra* shows that all phenomena within saṃsāra and nirvāṇa are primordially perfect, completely awakened, and inseparable as the nature of great purity and equality. The teaching is, therefore, not concerned with how certain causes and effects should be accepted or rejected. Neither does it explain the way to cultivate the causes for a buddhahood that results at a later time by relying on one's potential, a spiritual friend, and other such factors.

These points can also be understood from the brief presentation of the setting, where it says, "at the time when it is thus taught." The phrase "thus taught" indicates the indivisible realization of the teacher and his retinue. Likewise, there is a special reason for saying "at the time when it is" rather than "at one time it was."

In this way, the meaning of the words in the brief presentation of the setting should be explained by correlating them with three aspects: the outer aspect, the setting for the appearance of the tantra; the inner aspect, the array of the awakened mind; and the secret aspect, the principle of luminous wisdom. A detailed explanation of the five perfections begins with an account of how the maṇḍala of the natural and spontaneously present ground arises from the state of compassion and how the maṇḍalas of the peaceful and wrathful deities are then projected out from it. Such details can be learned from the elaborate exposition found in the commentary to the words and meaning of this vajra tantra.

2. The Prelude

Generally, in a prelude the teacher will encourage by smiling, emitting light, and extending his tongue, while the retinue will facilitate a discussion of the topic in question by making gestures and requests. However, in this extraordinary context the prelude involves the Thus-Gone One spontaneously addressing himself in a state of wonder. Thus, he elucidates the meaning of enlightenment to himself as the primordial maṇḍala of the purity and equality of all phenomena, the realization of the single sphere of enlightenment.

Moreover, as the aspect of skillful methods, Samantabhadra initiates the discussion by considering the magnificence of enlightenment as the original purity of all phenomena, in which their essential nature is one of bodies and wisdoms. Thus, by saying, "Amazing! The components of the vajra aggregates . . ." he points out, in short, that the world and its contents are a vast purity. This purity is spontaneously present within a state beyond characteristics. Thus, Samantabhadrī, as the aspect of knowledge, initiates the discussion by considering the magnificence of enlightenment within the great equality of the basic space of phenomena. With the statement, "The ten directions are empty, the realms primordially void," she points out, in short, the great equality of appearance and existence. The lord and consort, as the identity of means and knowledge beyond meeting and parting, initiate the discussion by considering the magnificence of enlightenment in the manner of the great perfection, the inseparable truths of purity and equality. Thus, in saying, "Amazing, wonderful, wondrous dharma . . ." they reveal, in short, the natural wisdom of the inseparable two truths.

Whether in the past, present, or future, no phenomenon has ever been, or will ever be, beyond this natural state. However, there are beings that fail to realize this state because they are separated from it by four secrets. For such beings, compassionate emanations manifest to teach. In this way, beings are guided by the infinite display of the magical net in whatever way is required. The six capable ones manifest in correspondence to the six classes of disciples. These six subsume all the various emanations. Since they harmonize with the constitutions, faculties, and inclinations that sentient beings possess, the various types of teaching that are given are limitless. Nevertheless, all teachings can be subsumed and explained in terms of the principles of the five vehicles, in combination with the wrathful approaches that are used to liberate the streams of being of negative individuals who are otherwise extremely hard to guide.

3. The Meaning of the Tantra

This section includes (1) a general presentation of the principles of the three continua and (2) a specific explanation of the path continuum. The first of these consists of explanations of (1) the ground continuum, (2) the path continuum, and (3) the fruition continuum.

1. The Ground Continuum
The ground continuum, or causal continuum, is what one must realize. This discussion covers four topics: (1) pointing out the natural maṇḍala of the ground, (2) how delusion arises when that maṇḍala is not realized, (3) how there is no departure from this nature, even during delusion, and (4) how delusion is reversed.

1. The Natural Maṇḍala of the Ground
On this topic, it is taught:

> Without bondage and liberation, these are the qualities
> Of primordial and spontaneously perfected buddhahood.

As this quote states, all phenomena that comprise appearance and existence are primordially pure as the maṇḍala of enlightened body, speech, and mind. Free from all characteristics, they are a great equality beyond distinctions and confines. This enlightened state is known as the "natural and spontaneously present maṇḍala of the ground." This is precisely what was explained in the context of the prelude. Within this essential state, no one has ever been bound and, therefore, no one is ever liberated. As it is free from all aspects of duality, it is also beyond limits and partiality. Present as the nature of the indivisible two truths, it is known as "the essential ground of the natural state."

When this ground is genuinely realized, it is nirvāṇa. When it goes unrealized, however, it is the ground of saṃsāra. It is called "ground" because it is the nature of all phenomena of saṃsāra and nirvāṇa without exception. Because it is continuously and immutably present in everyone, from sentient beings to buddhas, it is also called "continuum." The bodies and wisdoms of the final fruition manifest by virtue of actualizing the purity of this ground. For this reason, it is also termed the "causal continuum," in consideration of the way that it manifests.

It is with reference to the empty aspect of this very ground that the *Mother of the Victorious Ones* and other such scriptures speak of "the basic space of phenomena," "the perfectly authentic," and "suchness." In acknowledgment of its appearance as bodies and wisdoms, certain sūtras, such as those that point out the essence, refer to it as "the essence of the Thus-Gone One." Here, in the mantra vehicle of definitive meaning, it is referred to as "the identity of great purity and equality," "the inseparable truths of appearance and emptiness," and "the maṇḍala of the primordial ground."

A "thus-gone one" is referred to as such by virtue of having realized this ground just as it is, and who has thus gone forth, becoming of one taste with the natural state of suchness. Similarly, a "buddha" is one who has unfolded genuine wisdom regarding the meaning of the ultimate natural state. Any type of realization of this ground is termed "the path."

2. How Delusion Arises

When this very ground is not realized exactly as it is, it becomes polluted by temporary delusion. Thereby, the ground is experienced and conceived of in a mistaken way. This is known as the "constructed ground of delusion" and "impure appearance of delusion." Although the basic space of the original ground is primordially pure in essence, by nature it is inseparable from its own spontaneously present appearances; they are a unity. It is due to this crucial fact that buddhas manifest when the natural state is realized, whereas sentient beings manifest by failing to do so.

Generally speaking, what we call "mind" is something that is aware of objects. If this were not the case, delusion would be impossible, as would any realization of facts free from delusion. The natural disposition of the mind is to apprehend objects. It is, therefore, possible that the nature of an object may be apprehended correctly, perceiving a rope as a rope, for instance. However, if the mind is led astray by various circumstances, it may also perceive mistakenly, such as when a rope is seen as a snake. In the same way, the self-display that appears spontaneously due to the unimpeded radiance of primordial awareness may be apprehended as objects. From this seed of dualistic delusion, the appearances of existence then grow forth on a vast scale.

This state resembles water that has completely frozen into ice. From the perspective of someone who experiences and grasps onto all that may appear in an ordinary dualistic manner, the fact of great purity and equality is not evident. Because such a mistaken mind is in conflict with the way of wisdom, the reality of the nature that dwells as the ground becomes dormant and invisible. Instead, what appears is nothing but delusion.

While the way that this delusion obscures the natural state can be explained in infinite detail, it can also be summarized as the obscurations of the four states: (1) During the waking state, the cognitions of the six collections move crudely and with clarity toward their objects, apprehending various ordinary appearances. This obscures the nature of the emanation body, the complete purity of appearance and existence within the magical net. (2) While dreaming, what appears is merely the energetic mind. By fixating on the manifestation of these various insubstantial self-displayed experiences, one obscures the nature of the enjoyment body of self-displayed wisdom. (3) During deep sleep, the movements of the mind and mental states withdraw as one plunges into a dark state of utter oblivion. This obscures the nature of the nonconceptual dharma body. (4) At the time of immersion all coarse sensations are obliterated by the taste of bliss. Grasping and attachment within that state obscure the nature of the unified essence body.

Thus, wandering along in continuous delusion, one fails to see the reality of the four bodies that dwell within. These delusions could not possibly occur without a cause. One may, therefore, wonder what lies at their root. In the common vehicles, they are said to be rooted in the mental state of ignorance itself. In the tantras of mantra, however, they are described to be rooted in the subtle karmic energy that triggers dualistic perceptions in the mind. Alternatively, delusion is also described as the function of subtle semen, ovum, and energy—the predisposition for transference within the three experiences. Moreover, the extremely subtle root of this energetic mind is said to appear from the primordial and unceasing self-display. As such, one should understand that all explanations of the ground found in the various vehicles come down to the ground of the great perfection.

3. Delusion and the Natural Ground

Even as these appearances unfold, there is never any straying from the reality of the natural ground, just as a conch may appear to be yellow, while in fact its nature remains white. In the same way, all the phenomena that comprise appearance and existence are never beyond the nature of great purity and equality, regardless of whether this nature is realized or not. This is also expressed in the profound sūtras, which say: "Whether or not the thus-gone ones appear, the reality of all phenomena has been this way from the start."

4. The Reversal of Delusion

Just as light overcomes darkness, these forms of delusion are reversed by the functioning of either the actual and authentic wisdom that accords with the natural state, or the special knowledge that resembles it. Let us consider the experience of a beginner. Through study and contemplation, one may give rise to the special view of mantra that eliminates misconceptions concerning the natural state of the ground. However, although ordinary grasping may have diminished in his or her perception, ordinary experiences will still remain. This is similar to someone who infers that a conch is white and no longer considers it to be yellow, though he or she may still see it as such.

As one meditates in accordance with the meaning of the view and gradually becomes proficient on the path, one's deluded clinging to appearances will decrease, like ice melting into water, and pure vision will gradually unfold. Nevertheless, this state will still remain tainted. It is only when even the most subtle seeds of delusion have finally been eliminated that wisdom will be irreversibly dominant, like ice fully melted into water. These points are taught in the tantra, which proclaims: "Amazing! From the essence of the Bliss-Gone One..." and "Whatever phenomena of delusion there are in the world..."

These points can also be proven through ordinary reasoning. The *Commentary on Valid Cognition* explains:

> *Consciousness is a phenomenon*, or a nature, *that* is aware of and *apprehends objects*. From the perspective of the subject, *it is what apprehends* the object *exactly as it is. Moreover*, considering the object, *this* subjective cognition *is produced by the identity of* exactly *that which is present* in the essence of the object, since that object is what the cognition apprehends. *This is the nature*, or natural state, of subject and object. When *that* mind *strays* into error, it *is caused by other conditions*, such as the misconception of a permanent self and so forth.
>
> Still, such deviations are not corrected by themselves. *Their correction depends on the condition* of familiarity with the path that is brought forth by the valid cognitions that undermine them. Indeed, it is possible to correct this by certain conditions since

such deviations are adventitious and, therefore, *unstable*. Thus, they can be undermined by valid cognition, *just as the belief of* a rope being *a snake* can.

This being so, *the nature of mind is luminosity*, in the sense that it cannot be separated from the remedial factor of accurate perception. *The stains*, mistaken concepts, such as the view of a self and attachment, can be separated from the natural state precisely because they *are adventitious. Even before*, during periods of study and contemplation, *those* mistaken concepts *were unable* to impair the vision of the authentic meaning. It should, therefore, go without saying that *later*, once the cultivation of the path is complete, *they will not be able* to cause any harm *against the very identity*, or nature, *of this* remedial mind.

They do have a slight *ability* to damage a mind in which habitual tendencies have not yet been exhausted. *However, these* mistaken concepts *are unable to remain for long in that* mind, *which* is training and *has the essential ability to engender* in its own continuum *that* valid cognition *which impairs* such apprehension. When the continuum has been permeated by the authentic view, they are *just like* a *fire* that has been lit *on wet ground* and quickly dies out.

The mind that is *without torment* in the form of suffering *and in possession of the authentic meaning cannot* possibly *be reversed, even through persistent error*. This is *because the mind has assumed the perspective of that* reality. Hence, no valid cognition could possibly reverse it.

Similar explanations are to be found in other scriptures, such as the *Nondual Victory Tantra* and the *Ever-Excellent Means of Accomplishment*.

2. The Path Continuum
The explanation of the method that produces realization, or the path continuum, covers: (1) the essence of the path, (2) its divisions, and (3) how the path is traversed.

1. The Essence of the Path
The essence of the path is to understand the meaning of the ground continuum and correctly access its meaning. By the power of such practice, all the

temporary stains of delusion will be eliminated and the natural state will be actualized. In short, this essence is the wisdom of the five paths, including the retinue. The *Tantra of the Secret Essence* thus states:

> The retention that is applied to the characteristics of understanding
>   and application—
> The causes and conditions that ripen the result—
> These capable and powerful factors
> Are renowned as the field of the victorious knowledge holders.

It is by relying on, or following, this approach that the fruition is actualized. Hence, it is called the *path*. Moreover, this approach is the method that actualizes the objective and that which produces an understanding of the ground. It also allows one to achieve the fruition via a path that unfolds in a gradual and continuous process. Hence, it is also called *continuum*.

2. The Divisions of the Path

This section includes (1) a general explanation and (2) a detailed explanation. The general explanation covers (1) the division of two vehicles, (2) the demonstration of five vehicles, and (3) the presentation of nine vehicles.

1. The Two Vehicles

In the present context, the four common vehicles of renunciation, along with the three outer tantras, are termed "the long path," while the extraordinary vajra vehicle is known as "the shortcut to the fruition." These are the two divisions.

2. The Five Vehicles

Concerning the five-fold division, it is taught:

> The definitive emergence of the four vehicles
> Is the fruition of a single vehicle.

Thus, there are five vehicles: the vehicle of gods and humans, the vehicle of listeners, the vehicle of self-realized buddhas, the vehicle of bodhisattvas, and the unsurpassable vehicle of secret mantra.

1. The Vehicle of Gods and Humans

According to the tenets of the vehicle of gods and humans, one should adhere to the authentic mundane view of trusting in the definite consequences of one's actions. In this way, through practicing the ten virtues and the meditative absorptions of thought and form, one will be born as a human or god in the form and formless realms.

2. The Vehicle of the Listeners

In the tenets of the vehicle of the listeners, one must be disciplined and train in meditative absorption. The latter, moreover, should be in harmony with the view that correctly acknowledges the meaning of the four truths. Thereby, one will become accustomed to the absence of the personal self and achieve the seven temporary fruitions, such as becoming a stream enterer. As the final fruition, one will become a foe destroyer who has exhausted all bonds of the three realms. This vehicle contains two philosophical systems, those of the Proponents of Distinctions and the Sūtra Followers.

3. The Vehicle of Self-Realized Buddhas

The vehicle of self-realized buddhas is for those who have arrived at their final existence due to the strength of their past training. Without a spiritual friend, the power of reality allows them to realize the four truths through comprehending the profound principles of outer and inner dependent origination. In seeing the one-and-a-half-fold absence of self, they manifest as foe destroyers who are self-realized buddhas. Based on differences in the quality of their supportive faculties, and in their accumulations on the path, there are two fruitions: "those who live in groups" and "those who are rhinoceros-like."

4. The Vehicle of the Bodhisattvas

In the vehicle of the bodhisattvas, one engenders the twofold awakened mind through the approach of the undirected ultimate and the illusory relative. One then trains in the ten perfections and gains familiarity with the meaning of the twofold absence of self over three incalculable eons. It is held that this allows for the accomplishment of full and complete enlightenment. This vehicle contains both the Middle Way and Mind Only systems. While the former sees the complete absence of self, the latter asserts the reality of nondual self-awareness and, thus, fails to fully acknowledge the subtle absence of self of phenomena.

5. The Vehicle of Secret Mantra

In the vehicle of secret mantra, the maṇḍala of the final fruition itself is taken as the path in the present by means of various special views and modes of conduct. Through this method, complete buddhahood is quickly accomplished. There are two divisions in secret mantra: inner mantra and outer mantra. The first is practiced by means of considering oneself and the practiced deity to be equal and without any difference in terms of quality and identity. The second is practiced by considering oneself and the deity to be different in terms of the relative, both qualitatively and in terms of identity, and receiving the blessing of the deity in one's own stream of being.

Outer mantra contains three vehicles: (1) action tantra, (2) dual tantra, and (3) practice tantra. In action tantra, oneself and the deity are considered to be ultimately indistinguishable. In terms of the relative, however, the deity is held to be the perfection of all good qualities and that which confers blessings, similar to a master and servant. Simply seeing things in terms of superiority and inferiority is not what signifies this view's superiority. Instead, its superiority lies in the exceptional certainty that the two accomplishments are sure to be achieved in one's own stream of being by relying on deity and mantra, just as a master is able to grant great favors to his or her servants. Moreover, this is not just a matter of knowing that the deity can grant accomplishments. Rather, the certainty is exceptional because one becomes convinced that oneself and the deity are essentially indivisible in the end.

The key point, therefore, is to develop certainty about the unity that oneself and the deity are ultimately equal, while dependent origination is unfailing when it comes to the relative. Subsequently, one should practice the features of the deity in a genuine manner, such as its form and mantra, as they are taught in the scriptures. With such methods, one will swiftly become enlightened as the essence of the deity, like iron turned into gold through alchemy.

In this way, one lays the foundation by realizing the pure view. Then, in harmony with the view, one exerts oneself in the practice of deity, mantra, and meditative absorption. The fruition is accomplished by assembling these causes and conditions. By properly observing outer ritualistic aspects, such as cleansing and purification, emphasis is placed on physical and verbal conduct and great efforts are made to please the deity. Thereby, ordinary accomplishments, such as those of the knowledge holders of the desire and form realms, will be temporarily achieved through the power of the deity. Ultimately, the state of the bliss-gone ones of the three families will be accomplished within sixteen lifetimes.

In dual tantra, the view and realization are enhanced further. Consequently, oneself (as the samaya being) and the deity (as the wisdom being) are viewed as equals like siblings or friends. In harmony with this view, one then observes a conduct similar to kriyā tantra and practices a meditation similar to practice tantra. In this way, one achieves the accomplishments of a buddha of the four families within seven lifetimes. These are the assertions of the vehicle of ubhaya tantra, also known as dual tantra.

In the vehicle of practice tantra, certainty in the unity of the two truths develops tremendously. Through this, one develops the view that practice can take place in terms of oneself and the deity being inseparable, like water poured into water. In accordance with that view, one no longer depends on outer actions. Rather, one sees that accomplishment is achieved exclusively through inner practice and then applies the four seals of the buddha's body, speech, mind, and activity. By familiarization with this, buddhahood as the identity of the five classes is attained within three lifetimes.

In this way, the three outer tantras also take as their path the deity, whose nature is the fruitional bodies and wisdoms—the final perfection of purity—manifesting in the form of attributes and mantras. As such, in this approach various means are used to carry out the deeds of the buddhas in the present moment. In this capacity, they do indeed take the fruition as the path. Thus, their methods are superior and more swiftly accomplished when compared to the path of sūtra.

Next, we have the great practices of the unsurpassable vehicles of inner mantra. In these approaches, one realizes the profound view that oneself and the deity are primordially beyond meeting and parting and that all that appears and exists is pure and equal. In accordance with this view, one trains in the two profound stages and engages in actions that are free from anything to adopt or abandon, reveling in the pure intrinsic nature of whatever appears. It is held that this allows one to attain the identity of the four bodies and five wisdoms, the unified state beyond training, the great sixth vajra holder, in this present lifetime.

Inner mantra is further divided into (1) development, (2) completion, and (3) great perfection. Development refers to mahāyoga. Here, the ultimate fruition is enlightened body, speech, mind, qualities, and activity. As this is primordially beyond meeting with, or separating from, ultimate wisdom and ultimate basic space, together these are known as "the essential, spontaneous presence of the seven spheres of the ultimate." In short, basic space adorned with the bodies and wisdoms is emptiness endowed with all supreme aspects at the time of the fruition. This is the superior ultimate truth. As manifestations of this state, the appearances of the world and its inhabitants are by nature bodies and wisdoms that lack true establishment. This illusory wisdom is the superior relative truth. Thus, appearance and emptiness are beyond meeting and parting in the context of both truths. Furthermore, as the two truths include the purity of the bodies and wisdoms, they are superior to the common two truths.

In reality, both the appearances of the relative at the time of the ground and the path, and the appearances of the final ultimate at the time of the consummate fruition, are the indivisible essence of ground and fruition. This indivisibility of the two superior truths is viewed as the great dharma body. In sum, the union of basic space and the appearances of the bodies and wisdoms is the unity of appearance and emptiness. To complete the strength of meditation that accords with this state, one engages in the trainings of the three absorptions along with their auxiliary aspects. In this way, one traverses the path of the four knowledge holders and manifests enlightenment at the level of the great gathering of the wheel of syllables.

Completion refers to anuyoga. In this system, it is taught that the natural maṇḍala of the ground can be manifested by applying the key points of the indwelling channels, energies, and essences of the vajra body, without relying on the path of outer elaboration and efforts. Its essence is the maṇḍala of awakened mind, the Child of Great Bliss, which is the indivisibility of the maṇḍala of Samantabhadrī, the basic space of emptiness, and the maṇḍala of Samantabhadra, the means of bliss. To ascertain this to be the universal master of all buddha families and maṇḍalas is the view of the inseparability of bliss and emptiness. In harmony with this view, one then trains in the practices related to one's own body and the body of another, pursuing a path that emphasizes the wisdom of great bliss. Once the end of the five paths has been reached, one will accomplish the unified state beyond training.

According to atiyoga, the nature of the natural state itself is primordial self-aware awakening. Within the state of the indivisible primordially pure essence and spontaneously present nature, the apparent expression of compassion manifests unceasingly. Without having to utilize methods that require effort, such as development and the binding of the energies, this intrinsic nature of the three bodies is ascertained through nonaction and self-clarity, in which there is nothing to dispose of or retain. This is the innate view of empty awareness. In accordance with this view, one trains in the four ways of resting freely according to cutting through and the four lamps according to direct crossing. Thereby, one perfects the path of the four visions and becomes self-liberated within primordial and spontaneously present basic space.

Here, the categories of the five vehicles and their subdivisions have been presented. The tenet systems that pertain to these vehicles can also be condensed into five. The first of these, the correct mundane tenets, assert that the effects of actions do not go to waste.

Second are the tenets of the vehicle of characteristics. This system asserts that all the outer and inner phenomena that comprise the apprehended and apprehender arise in the manner of dependent origination. Because this is misapprehended, one erroneously misconstrues a person and the like. This delusion, however, dissolves once one realizes that there is no personal self or self of phenomena, neither as outer apprehended object, nor as an apprehending mind. This, in turn, brings about the actualization of nirvana. Since the degree of realization may vary, this vehicle is divided into three systems, those of the listeners, the Mind Only, and the Middle Way, respectively.

Third are the tenets of the three outer tantras. These teach that deluded experience and the appearances of dependent origination do indeed arise as the unfailing result of karmic actions. By relying on an abundance of means that pertain to deity and mantra, however, one will swiftly be granted freedom from these factors and become untainted by the actions of existence and their effects.

Fourth are the general tenets of the unsurpassable practice. This approach acknowledges that suffering itself is enlightenment and that disturbing emotions are themselves the great wisdom of complete liberation. When training on the path subsequent to this realization, one will remain untainted by karmic actions and their effects.

Fifth are the consummate tenets of the great perfection. This system teaches that all phenomena of saṃsāra and nirvāṇa are spontaneously present as great purity and equality and that they have been this way from the very beginning. Therefore, one is primordially untainted by the fetters of ordinary actions and their effects, independently of any effort on the path. Among all the various paths, this alone is the ultimate.

The *Tantra of the Secret Essence* teaches these points in the passage that begins, "All of these appearances of outer and inner interdependence . . ." In commenting on this passage, Rongzom and Longchenpa differ slightly. The concise explanation that I have offered here is, however, in agreement with both.

3. The Nine Vehicles
The liberating paths of the supramundane vehicles explained above can also be classified into nine vehicles: the three vehicles that guide through renunciation (the vehicles of the listeners, self-realized buddhas, and bodhisattvas), the three vehicles of Vedic austerities (kriyā, ubhaya, and yoga), and the three vehicles of mastery in means (mahā, anu, and ati).

The assertion that these approaches do not involve distinct views occurs from a failure to distinguish between the view and the object of the view, and between the views of sūtra and mantra. As the subject that ascertains the inseparability of the two truths becomes increasingly sublime, one cannot deny that various views exist in terms of the relative, such as that of master and servant. If the relative subject did not entail a view, the consequence would be that a) the authentic mundane view, b) the view that realizes the features of the four truths (with the exception of emptiness and absence of self), and c) the view that accurately ascertains conventional objects, are not views at all. No one would posit the principles of the path in such a way.

It may then be argued that these are indeed views, yet, since the subject that holds them is not ultimate, these differences are not sufficient to delineate the superiority of a particular vehicle. Nevertheless, the ascertainment of the relative develops based on the degree to which clarity in the experience of the ultimate has been achieved. Thus, this is sufficient to prove such superiority.

Likewise, it may be argued that viewing deities in terms of the relative cannot be a view, since teachings on the nonexistence of buddhas and sentient beings pertain to the view, whereas teachings that speak of their existence relate to meditation. However, this is a very awkward position to maintain. What we are concerned with here is not simply the view that there is no cold on the ground where fire burns, nor can we equate this to imagining oneself to be a lion when frightened by a dog. Instead, it is the view and meditation of the authentic path that allow one to relinquish the two obscurations and achieve the final unchanging fruition. As such, in the present context, view and meditation must be "awareness with legs." Meditation that lacks the certainty of the view and views that are divorced from the practice of meditation are like looking east while going west. All paths that connect with the way things are and all subjective cognitions of the two truths are definitely preceded by the authentic view because genuine ascertainment is produced through valid cognition. Moreover, statements of existence and nonexistence are made from the perspectives of examining the conventional and the ultimate, respectively. Therefore, since the consequence of the above position would be that no meditation could be concerned with the ultimate and that nothing that is conventional could be ascertained through valid cognition, this position is wholly impractical. It must, therefore, be understood that there are two types of view. One is the *view that regards the subject*, which is ascertained through valid cognitions that investigate the conventional. Another is the *view that regards reality*, which is ascertained by valid cognitions that investigate the ultimate.

Likewise, the tradition of classifying atiyoga as wisdom but not a vehicle is a difficult position to maintain. Generally, both the wisdom of the path and the wisdom of the fruition are vehicles. This is generally acknowledged in scriptures that speak of "the vehicle in which one is transported by this cause" and "the vehicle in which one is transported within this result." In particular, since atiyoga is the ultimate wisdom of the path of unsurpassable mantra, it is the king of all vehicles. The very scriptures that emphasize atiyoga, moreover, are the summit of all vehicles.

In this way there are various ways of expanding or condensing the number of vehicles since they are taught in consideration of the diverse mind-sets of those in need of guidance. Thus, while one may distinguish between two, three, or more vehicles, the presentation here is exhaustive. As this is the case, this tantra is a universal scripture.

2. The Path of Unsurpassable Mantra

The specific explanation of the path of unsurpassable mantra includes an explanation of development and completion from the perspective of the essence and an explanation of means and liberation in terms of practice. The first section includes discussions of both development and completion.

1. Development

Accessing the purity and equality of appearance and existence through conceptual creations and training in accord with the view that ascertains the meaning of the natural continuum of the ground is known as "development stage practice." It is also known in other scriptures as "the practice of inference" or "the path of fabrication." The development stage is practiced in five levels that correspond to the stages of saṃsāric development. These five levels are great emptiness, illusory compassion, the single form, the elaborate form, and the practice of group gathering. Downwardly, this practice purifies the habitual tendencies of cyclic existence. Upwardly, it perfects the fruition of the transcendence of suffering. It also matures one for the practice of the completion stage. In short, with this approach training continues until one is able to create the perception that appearance and existence are an all-pervasive purity, the wheel of the magical net. This perfection of the development stage is known as "the development stage of appearance and existence manifesting as the ground."

Generally speaking, development stage practice by itself can lead to the attainment of all mundane accomplishments, up to those of the Unexcelled Realm. It will not, however, lead to the actualization of the transcendent path. Still, by perfecting this profound approach of the unity of development and completion, the perception of the true meaning will be naturally induced by the completion stage. There is nothing illogical in asserting this, just as the path of sūtra is also capable of inducing a vision of the true meaning after a long duration. Moreover, someone who has perfected the four practices is also able to engage without difficulty in certain advanced practices. This includes the approach of isolating the mind and observing the nāda in the heart center, as taught in the *Gathering of Secrets*, as well as utilizing the various key points of the subtle essences that are taught in the different classes of tantra, that is, empty forms, the wisdom seal, and the completion stage of uncontrived natural rest. The development stage can also be either elaborate or concise, or divided in relation to the progression of tantric ritual.

2. Completion

In the completion stage, the profound methodical pith instructions actualize the tantra of the ground, the great purity and equality that dwells within as the maṇḍala of spontaneous presence. For this reason, it is termed "completion stage," "the practice of direct perception," and "the path of the innate." Although the completion stage contains many divisions, they can all be condensed into two categories: (1) the application of the key points of the support (the channels, energies, and essences) through yogic exercises, vase-breathing, the blissful melting of the subtle essence, and so forth; and (2) the application of the key points of the supported (the essence of luminosity), such as the practice of empty forms or direct crossing. In short, various methods for actualizing the wisdoms of the four vajras are taught in the tantras, including the "five stages" and "six unions."

In terms of how they are practiced, all teachings, whether they are complete or partial, can be divided into two categories: (1) the *path with characteristics*, which is based on keeping an object in mind and applying physical and verbal effort and (2) the *path without characteristics*, which is effortless. In terms of what is practiced, there are three divisions: (1) luminosity, the wisdom of the empty; (2) illusory body, the wisdom of appearance; and (3) the wisdom of the unity of these two. All completion stage practices are nothing more than ways of actualizing pure wisdom by allowing the karmic energies to dissolve into the central channel, though this may be brought about either directly or indirectly.

In this tantra, the completion stage with signs is taught via the instructions on the practice of the subtle essences that relate to the four wheels, as well as the path of means, which includes both the gradual path of the upper gate and the instantaneous path of the lower gate. The completion stage without signs, on the other hand, is taught through the pith instructions of the luminous great perfection.

In this way, the path of these two stages clears away impurities, through which the natural state is actualized. However, if the natural state were not pure by nature, then the development stage would be a mental creation that conflicts with the natural state. Moreover, when certain practices, such as arresting the karmic energies within one's ordinary body, cause the accomplished entities to appear as deities in one's own experience, then that would be a deluded experience. Like a magic stone appearing to be a horse or an elephant, this would not accord with the way things are. Such an apprehension would be an erroneous cognition. The same thing would then also hold for taking the five poisons as the path and having a conduct free of acceptance and rejection. If this were the case, claiming such a path to be superior to the path of sūtra would be astonishing indeed!

If the difference between sūtra and mantra lay only in skillful means and not in the view, then why would such easy and efficacious means not be taught in the sūtras as well? One must understand that it is because the view of the spontaneous presence of cause and effect is absent in the causal vehicles that those who adhere to those vehicles are not yet ready for such methods. There are some who assert that sentient beings can be forcefully transformed into buddhas through methods alone, without their understanding the state of great primordial purity and equality. Those who say this, however, are unable to establish the two stages as a path that accords with the way things are. Hence, one must understand that these statements severely denigrate the vehicle of mantra.

2. Means and Liberation
This section discusses the path of definitive means and the path of liberation through knowledge.

1. The Path of Means
The *Tantra of the Secret Essence* states:

> This amazing, magical, wondrous dharma
> Does not arise from some other place.
> It arises within the state
> Of knowledge itself, supported by means.

As noted here, the emphasis of this path is the forceful manifestation of one's own inner wisdom through wondrous skillful activity. This, in turn, results in the swift accomplishment of the fruition, just as iron is instantly transformed into gold through the application of makṣika [pyrite]. First and foremost, this involves two factors: engendering blissful wisdom through blazing and dripping in relation to the six wheels and engendering the melting bliss of unchanging wisdom through the descent, retention, reversal, and pervasion that pertains to the union with the secret space. As a subsidiary aspect of that, this also includes the various modes of conduct that pertain to the yogic discipline of great bliss.

During equipoise, when a diligent person relies on skillful means, he or she will come to experience the meaning, in various ways, that should be realized. This meaning is the continuum of the ground, within which the two truths are indivisible; it is a state free from thought and beyond conceptual mind. During the ensuing attainment, the power of such experiences automatically induces the certainty that all of appearance and existence are great purity and equality. The energies that carry thought, as well as the coarse and subtle

28   LUMINOUS ESSENCE

elements that are its conditions, are restrained by relying on the key points of the channels. This process causes concepts and their mount to dissolve into the blissful and empty basic space of the dhūtī, since it is the intrinsic nature of things that the mind will be naturally bound once the moving energies have been restrained. As the constitution of the elements and channels are purified, the energetic mind within the four wheels becomes workable and the knots on the central channel are untied. When that occurs, the appearances of wisdom gradually evolve, all the habitual tendencies for transference are reversed, and the vajra body of great bliss of the final fruition is attained.

2. The Path of Liberation

The *Tantra of the Secret Essence* states:

> Through a combination of studying, contemplating, and meditating on
> The maṇḍala of perfect wisdom
> The self-occurring and all-fulfilling are spontaneously present.

As stated here, the emphasis of this path is exceptional study, contemplation, and meditation, which lead to a decisive insight into the spontaneously perfected great maṇḍala, in which all phenomena are primordially enlightened as self-occurring wisdom. By training in this insight, one traverses the path and reaches liberation within the great equality of the maṇḍala of the self-manifest bodies and wisdoms, just as stone will turn into gold when in close proximity to the kaustubha jewel.

In this context there are two paths: The *instantaneous path* is for the most gifted individuals, for whom realization and familiarization are simultaneous. On the *gradual path*, the view is first resolved and then, in accordance with its meaning, the strength of absorption is developed. *Devoted training* involves a mere meditation on general features, without having perfected absorption. This produces the ability to actualize the genuine path in one's stream of being and carries the benefit of accomplishing various temporary activities. *Definitive perfection* refers to a path where meditation is perfected in the five gradual practices, such as great emptiness, as they pertain to the stages of death, the intermediate state, and birth. Based on this path, one actualizes the levels of the four knowledge holders.

In this way, an intelligent person will correctly ascertain the meaning of great purity and equality through study and contemplation. First, this exceptional view is ascertained. Then, in accordance with the view, one engages in the practices of equipoise and ensuing attainment that enable one to cultivate the meditative absorption of the path, whereby ordinary deluded thoughts are self-liberated. It is the nature of things that, once the thinking mind is liberated, the transference of the energy element, which is inextricably intertwined with the mind, will also be liberated into the basic space of wisdom. Thus, as the thoughts of dualistic deluded appearances and their conditions are self-pacified and self-liberated, the truth of the natural state will become evident and one will arrive at the fruition beyond training.

The paths of means and liberation are classified as such based on their respective emphasis of means and knowledge. This is not to say, however, that either of these is devoid of the other. Rather, one should understand that these two are equivalent, in the sense that both allow one to see the nature of the natural state.

In the context of group practice, the merely symbolic, illustrative wisdom may arise in the stream of being of the practitioner in accordance with his or her capacity, and one may become a knowledge holder of the desire or form realms. At the very least, one will gain various forms of accomplishment since one will have connected with the unique practice of the profound means of mantra.

In the case of genuine group practice on the path of definitive perfection, the supreme accomplishment is attained and the entire gathering proceeds to the levels of the knowledge holders. This occurs because smoke and the rest of the ten signs are complete, even when practicing the absorption of great emptiness in an authentic manner. Moreover, the practitioner who has accomplished the development stage of appearance and existence as manifest ground will arrive at the luminosity of the fourfold emptiness during equipoise and emerge from that state in the divine form of the mere energetic mind. Furthermore, during the ensuing attainment, the potential for the infinite appearances of all-pervasive purity will be perfected. Therefore, at the occasion of great accomplishment during the group practice, one relies on the proximate cause of a seal and thereby actualizes the truth of reality.

3. Traversing the Path

In this section, the teaching concerns the nature of the path to be traversed, the unsurpassable entrance gate to the fruition of consummate liberation.

This path can be divided into the five paths of unsurpassable mantra. The process of traversing this path is initiated by a person who possesses the most sublime, great compassion, wishing to accomplish the level of buddhahood in this very life to liberate all of the infinite number of sentient beings without exception. Understanding, moreover, that the path that leads to the final fruition depends exclusively on this vajra vehicle, the practitioner will thoroughly mature his or her stream of being by receiving the four ripening empowerments from a qualified master. The next step is to correctly observe the general, particular, and additional samayas and, in accordance with the authentic view of appearance and existence as great purity and equality, train correctly on the path of the two stages. Through this, one will gradually complete the five paths.

To begin, one meditates in accordance with the original purity of one's own and others' bodies as the maṇḍala circle and settles the mind in unity with the great equality of emptiness beyond concept. This is the application of mindfulness to the body. Transforming concepts of sensation into the wisdom of great bliss is the application of mindfulness to sensation. Binding all of the mind's constructs and mental states within the innate basic space of the luminous nature of mind is the application of mindfulness to the mind. Enjoying all phenomena of saṃsāra and nirvāṇa—all that appears and all that is imputed—as purity and equality without accepting or rejecting is the application of mindfulness to phenomena. This is how they are taught in the sacred tantra of the *Magical Net*.

The superiority of the great vehicle's applications of mindfulness to those of the lesser vehicle is mentioned in *Distinguishing the Middle from Extremes*:

> In the case of the bodhisattva,
> Focus, directing the mind,
> And attainment are superior.

Mantra is superior to sūtra in a similar way. In the mantra approach, one focuses on one's own body, the bodies of others, and so forth. In short, one focuses on all the phenomena of saṃsāra and nirvāṇa while directing the mind to their inseparability from primordial great purity and equality. This enables one to attain the final fruition without having to go through other paths.

Therefore, while on the path of sūtra, in terms of the relative one rejects saṃsāra and accepts nirvāṇa. Here, however, one pursues the path by uniting with the inseparability of saṃsāra and nirvāṇa. This leads to mantra's lesser path of accumulation, which has the nature of the four applications of mindfulness. This then evolves into the intermediate path of accumulation, the nature of which is the four correct relinquishments, and then the greater path of accumulation, the nature of which is the four bases of miraculous power. Thus, on the path of accumulation, the meaning of the inseparable two truths of purity and equality is primarily encountered as a mere object of intellectual understanding by means of study and contemplation. It is called the "path of accumulation" because, in this context, one exerts oneself in development and completion, thereby causing the path of the noble ones to manifest within one's stream of being.

As one's practice of development and completion develops further, meditation experience becomes the most important factor. The four stages of the path of joining then occur once the illustrated, the actual natural state, is encountered through an object universal. On the path of joining, the stage of heat occurs when the illustrative example-wisdom first arises as an early indication of the fire-like wisdom of the path of seeing. This also has the nature of the five faculties—the faculty of knowledge that realizes the natural state of the inseparable truths of purity and equality, assisted by faith and the other faculties. When this develops even further, the realization of the stage of summit occurs on the path of joining. This stage is reached when the five faculties, such as faith, manifest as the summit of all the vacillating roots of virtue, yet remain unable to become powers. The stage of acceptance on the path of joining arises in one's stream of being when the five faculties of the stage of summit can no longer be overcome by their individual discordant factors, and therefore become of the nature of the five powers. This stage is so called because here the mind becomes resilient due to a unique experience of the natural state of reality. When this develops further, the final symbolic wisdom, which is capable of directly inducing actual wisdom, manifests within one's stream of being. This is the stage of the supreme property. It is referred to as such because this is supreme among all mundane paths and is able to induce the noble path. The path of joining receives its name because these stages connect with the path of seeing.

The path of joining is delineated by whether or not the symbolic wisdom has arisen in one's stream of being. However, at times it is explained that the development stage pertains to the path of accumulation, while the completion stage, such as vajra recitation, is practiced on the path of joining. Still, while this is the case for the gradual type of person, it is not categorically so. For example, it is possible that someone may recognize wisdom while receiving empowerment, whereby realization and familiarity occur instantaneously. Moreover, it is also possible to practice development and completion as a unity from the very start. It may also be the case that the symbolic wisdom can be induced through the profound development stage, in which one understands appearance and emptiness to be like the moon reflected in water. Finally, it is also possible that someone trains in certain practices, such as the vajra recitation, but still remains on the mere path of accumulation due to an inability to bring forth the symbolic wisdom. Therefore, no matter what approach one takes when practicing development and completion, as taught in their respective classes of tantra, the essential point is the fact that "the mantric path of joining" occurs when the symbolic wisdom arises in one's stream of being.

This symbolic wisdom takes two forms. The symbolic wisdom that occurs on the first two stages of the path of joining is an approximation, and comparable to a painting of the moon. On the second two stages it is genuine, and, hence, similar to a reflection of the moon in water.

The final realization of the path of joining induces the path of seeing. At this stage, one beholds the actual wisdom that is illustrated, which is comparable to the actual moon in the sky, without the duality of subject and object. In this way, one gains an actual realization of the seven aspects of the path of enlightenment, such as the knowledge that directly perceives the truth of reality.

The mantric path of cultivation occurs next. This path has the nature of the eight aspects of the noble path, such as the authentic view that directly witnesses appearance and existence as great purity and equality. It encompasses the nine grounds that relate to the elimination of nine obscurations. First, the second ground is achieved when the wisdom of the path of training arises in one's stream of being. This wisdom serves to remedy the most dominant of those factors that are discarded through cultivation. This gradually continues until the wisdom of the path of training finally reaches a point of culmination at the end of the continuum of the attainment of the tenth ground. This serves to remedy the least dominant factors that are discarded through cultivation.

At this point, one enters the consummate path and achieves equipoise within the final, natural state through the vajra-like absorption. Through the power of this absorption, even the subtlest potentials of the two obscurations are uprooted. Once they are, the supreme fruition is immediately achieved on the path of liberation and one awakens to buddhahood within the utterly pure wisdom body of the unified state beyond training.

The names of the grounds are the same as in the vehicle of the perfections. Their individual qualities and signs as well can be ascertained from the presentation offered in the scriptures. In this regard, there is no distinction between sūtra and mantra.

These five paths are presented with reference to the way one perceives the intrinsic nature of equality, meaning the actual luminosity, or the way things are. Thus, on the path of accumulation, luminosity is merely an object that one comes to understand through study and contemplation. On the path of joining, example luminosity is present, while actual luminosity manifests on the path of seeing. On the path of cultivation, the luminosity of training manifests, and on the path beyond training, the final luminosity itself occurs.

There are no differences between the grounds of the noble ones in terms of how the basic field of phenomena is directly perceived. However, there are major differences when it comes to how clear this experience has become. Still, these differences are experienced individually by the noble ones. They cannot be appreciated by a mind that is involved in study and contemplation, just as one cannot perceive the path of a bird flying in the sky. Nevertheless, the differences between the ten grounds can be proven in terms of how the certainty of the ensuing attainment manifests based on the attainment of clear experience, and how the qualities of abandonment and realization gradually evolve.

As the clear experience of reality continues to develop, the perception of the purity of appearance and existence also undergoes a process of transformation. Hence, we speak of the imaginary divine body on the path of accumulation, the divine body of the energetic mind on the path of joining, the divine body of luminosity on the path of seeing, the divine body of the union of training on the path of cultivation, and, finally, the divine body of the unified state beyond training. In these two ways, the path allows one to resolve the meaning of great purity and equality.

The so-called "unified state beyond training" is when the meaning of the inseparable truths of purity and equality manifest simultaneously, not in alternation. This is the ground of buddhahood. As this is the wisdom body of the indivisible two truths, this ground is essentially without divisions. Nevertheless, in consideration of the three bodies, the ground can be divided into the grounds of Universal Illumination, the Lotus Realm, and the Great Gathering of the Wheel of Syllables.

Although there are different ways to explain how these grounds relate to the three bodies, these explanations do not conflict with one another in terms of meaning. They all agree that these grounds do not differ in terms of abandonment and realization, but are merely conceptual distinctions. Other categorizations, such as the grounds of Great Bliss and Unsurpassed Wisdom, can be understood in the same manner.

When these grounds and paths are considered in the context of the path of means, the qualities of the five paths are seen to be the fruition of the energetic mind that dwells within the five wheels becoming increasingly workable. Moreover, the wisdom of the eleventh ground manifests once the twenty-one knots that the right and left channels form around the central channel are undone, as is well known in the general tantras of the mantra tradition.

The grounds and paths of mantra are generally divided in terms of causal and resultant grounds. With respect to their enumeration, distinctive names, and other such factors, they are treated differently in the various tantras. Even if we consider the four joys alone, we will find various presentations, such as the way these four correlate with the five paths. Nevertheless, this present account allows us to see that all the various explanations that pertain to the progression of the path, without exception, present the same key issue.

The relationship between this path and the four knowledge holders is discussed in a number of ways. According to the Great Omniscient One, the mind matures in deity practice at the end point of the path of inspired conduct, but the body has yet to transform into anything other than a matured form. However, the body of the great seal will be attained on the path of seeing as soon as one is free from the encasement of the body. This is the *matured knowledge holder*. Starting from the path of seeing, on the path of training, the body of maturation is transformed into a vajra body. The level of buddhahood can be reached without relinquishing such a body, as it is free of the defilement of the aggregates and possesses the vision of wisdom. This is the *knowledge holder with power over longevity*. For a noble one on the superior path of training, the body transforms into the deity that one has meditated on, and one's activity comes to resemble that of a buddha.

However, since all obscurations have yet to be exhausted, the actual, final fruition is not achieved at this point. This is the *knowledge holder of the great seal*. Finally, once abandonment and realization have been perfected, the stage beyond training is actualized. This is the *spontaneously present knowledge holder*.

The oral tradition of the Zur clan explains that all four knowledge holders pertain to the grounds of training of the noble ones. Someone who sees the truth of reality, yet lacks the mental capacity required to purify the defilements of the body with the fire of wisdom, is a *matured knowledge holder*. When the capacity to purify has been achieved and the body is immortal and pure, one is a *knowledge holder with power over longevity*. Thus, this tradition explains that there are two versions of the path of seeing. To continue, someone on the path of cultivation who possesses a body of illusory wisdom is a *knowledge holder of the great seal*. Finally, at the completion of the path of training, one is not yet a buddha. Nevertheless, one assumes the appearance of a vajra holder with the five bodies spontaneously present. This is referred to as the *spontaneously present knowledge holder*.

Etymologically speaking, the term "knowledge holder" is a translation of the Sanskrit word *vidyādhara*. *Vidyā* means "knowledge." More specifically, this refers to the nature of knowledge and wisdom that is the essential reality of mantra. *Dhara* means "to hold," thus implying that this reality is held and possessed within one's stream of being.

However these four knowledge holders are delineated, there is no conflict, as is the case with the four aspects of approach and accomplishment. These terms, moreover, can also be used in regard to the accomplishment of mantra. This is the case with the knowledge holders of the desire and form realms, and the sword knowledge holder. There is also a threefold classification of knowledge holders in terms of entering, dwelling on, and maturing the grounds. With respect to the path of cultivation alone, five knowledge holders are presented: those of the vajra, wheel, jewel, lotus, and sword. In this way, there are a number of different classifications.

3. The Fruition Continuum
The continuum of the final fruition is taught as follows:

> Actualized in the mind of the victors of the three times,
> The essence of supreme accomplishment

Is an inexhaustible, wish-fulfilling treasury,
Manifesting without increase or decrease.

Likewise:

Beyond one and many,
Suchness has neither limit nor center.
Not even seen by the buddhas,
Self-occurring wisdom manifests without abiding.

As well as:

The dharma body, unfathomable and indescribable...

Thus, the power of cultivating the path uproots all adventitious stains along with their predispositions and actualizes the natural maṇḍala of the ground exactly as it is, great indivisible purity and equality. This vajra-like body is the essence of the single sphere of self-occurring wisdom, the fully perfect enlightenment within the indivisibility of all phenomena. Its nature is one of permanent and pervasive great bliss. It is the master of the universal manifestation of inconceivable qualities and the embodiment of the final fruition—the unified state beyond training.

Its distinctive qualities can be summarized as the nature of the twenty-five fruitional qualities. There are five each for enlightened body, speech, mind, qualities, and activities. These can all be subsumed in the threefold principle of supportive body, supported wisdom, and performed enlightened activity. When elaborated upon, however, there is an array of distinct qualities that surpasses the imagination, equaling all aspects of the objects of knowledge that entirely fill the basic space of phenomena. For as long as space remains, these qualities bring benefit and happiness to sentient beings in a permanent, pervasive, and spontaneously present manner.

Why is this referred to as the continuum of fruition? It is known as *fruition* because it is the final and unsurpassable goal and because, in terms of the way things appear, it is actualized by the power of the path clearing away adventitious stains. It is referred to as *continuum* because it is never interrupted.

2. Specific Explanation of the Path Continuum
This section has two divisions: a demonstration of the various classification schemes and explaining the present context.

1. Various Classification Schemes
The tantras, as well as the commentaries on their intent, teach a number of classifications of the path of the vajra vehicle. Though the path of secret mantra can be taught as a single practice of indivisible means and knowledge, it can also be explained in a dual manner as development and completion, or means and knowledge. There are also threefold divisions, such as the practices of enlightened body, speech, and mind; view, meditation, and conduct; or approach, accomplishment, and activity. One fourfold division is based on gradual practices that take the wisdoms of the four vajras as the path, while another such division is made from the perspective of taking the buddha's enlightened body, speech, mind, and deeds as the path, in which case one speaks of binding with the ties of the four seals—the great seal, dharma seal, samaya seal, and action seal. Finally, there is also an explanation that condenses the entire path into five categories: empowerment, samayas, view, accomplishment, and enlightened activity.

Alternatively, according to the *Fortress Garland*, secret mantra can be explained in terms of six parameters:

> Samayas maintain the foundation, the view resolves, action determines, empowerment brings progression, absorption brings practical experience, and the key instructions accomplish the meaning.

According to the *Parkhab*, there is also a sevenfold classification into view, conduct, absorption, empowerment, samayas, enlightened activity, and accomplishment. Adding maṇḍala to these seven, there are eight.

According to Rongzom, the basis consists of five factors: maṇḍala, samayas, accomplishment, empowerment, and enlightened activity. There are also four subsidiary factors: mantra, mudrā, absorption, and offering, making a nine-fold classification. Since view and conduct pervade all of these, they are not listed separately.

There is also a tenfold division. These ten topics of tantra consist of the view, conduct, maṇḍala, empowerment, samayas, offerings, mantra, absorption, enlightened activity, and accomplishment. These ten embody all paths. Here, mantra and mudrā are combined into one category.

In this way, all these classifications offer proper explanations by emphasizing their respective topics, while showing other divisions to be subsidiary. Nevertheless, there is no difference between them in the sense that they are all able to explain the path of secret mantra in a comprehensive manner.

2. The Present Context

The presentation that concerns us in the present context is that of our own tradition. This excellent explanation is framed around an extensive categorization of eleven topics, or parameters, of tantra. These eleven are (1) the view of reality, (2) unmoving absorption, (3) determined action, (4) arranged maṇḍala, (5) progressive empowerment, (6) unbroken samayas, (7) zealous practice, (8) directed offerings, (9) activity display, (10) binding mudrā, and (11) recited mantra. These are enumerated in accordance with the eleven grounds.

1. View

Next, we shall offer an individual explanation of these points. First is the view.

> The single cause and the manner of syllables,
> Blessings and in actuality—
> By virtue of these four forms of perfect realization,
> Everything is the great king of the truly perfect.

As expressed in this verse, the view of great purity and equality is the precursor to all paths of unexcelled mantra. All other trainings must follow this view. The view is, therefore, of the utmost importance and will be explained in some detail. The view will be explained in terms of its (1) essence, (2) divisions, (3) principles, and (4) purpose.

1. Essence

The nature of the view is taught in terms of a common, general explanation and an extraordinary, specific explanation.

1. The Common, General Explanation

The term "view" derives from the Sanskrit word *dṛṣṭi*. It refers to a mind that definitively and decisively apprehends a cognized object once knowledge has eliminated misconception. Among the different kinds of knowledge, there are various levels of mundane and supramundane views, depending on whether or not an object is correctly ascertained.

The *Tantra of the Secret Essence* says:

> Not understanding and wrong understanding,
> Partial understanding and no understanding of the genuine,
> Discipline, intent, secret,
> And the naturally secret meaning.
> All of these are fully illustrated by statements,
> Based on assembled words formed by letters and sounds.
> The concealed meaning is revealed from within,
> And dwells in the enlightened mind of the vajra teacher.

As stated here, the view grows increasingly sublime. This process begins with the view of ordinary worldly people. In the absence of any philosophical investigation, such individuals believe that self and phenomena truly exist, just as they appear. The supreme view is only reached in the system of the glorious *Secret Essence*, which genuinely proves appearance and existence to be great purity and equality, the natural maṇḍala of the ground.

2. The Extraordinary, Specific Explanation

This system of the unexcelled vehicle is the pinnacle of all views, the ultimate philosophical position, and the ultimate destination of all paths. The extraordinary view of this system is the ascertainment of appearance and existence as great purity and equality. Furthermore, since a "view" is posited as having the character of identifying the meaning of that which is to be resolved, it must be primarily classified as a certainty related to the ensuing attainment. Equipoise, such as on the path of seeing, is described as "knowledge" and "wisdom"; only rarely is it referred to as a "view." However, since it does indeed behold the nature of reality, referring to it as a "view" does not present any problem.

Nevertheless, the manner in which the basic space of phenomena is observed during the equipoise of the noble ones is through individual self-awareness. As such, it transcends being an object of names and concepts. Still, the way in which clear experience is attained during equipoise naturally leads to certainty in the ensuing attainment. The individual levels and correct views of the noble ones are classified based on the certainty of the ensuing attainment. This is expressed in certain statements, such as "the universally present meaning, the supreme meaning."

Similarly, here one will rest in equipoise in the meaning of the great simplicity of unity. This equipoise, moreover, occurs due to the power of wisdom being transferred during empowerment, as well as one's meditation on the unique path. Thereby, appearance and existence are ascertained as great purity and equality during the ensuing attainment. This special view of mantra is a unique ascertainment of the meaning of the two truths since it is proved by the power of fact.

2. Divisions

As is widely discussed in the various classes of tantra of the ancient translations, there are three different views: (1) the view that observes the subject, (2) the view that observes reality, and (3) the view that observes self-awareness. These three are synonymous with the conventional subject, the ultimate subject, and the subject that ascertains the indivisibility of the two truths. Hence, these three are not only pertinent to this discussion but encompass all views.

The three divisions presented in this context, however, are quite extraordinary. The view that observes phenomena sees the world and its inhabitants as great purity, the maṇḍala of bodies and wisdoms of the support and the supported. The view that observes reality views all phenomena as the indivisible great equality. Finally, the view that observes self-awareness is the individual self-awareness of the superior truth of indivisible purity and equality—the great dharma body.

3. Establishing the View through Reasoning

This explanation involves (1) proving how the mantric view is superior to the view of sūtra and (2) proving the profundity of the view of the exceedingly sublime mantra.

1. The Superiority of the Mantric View

One might wonder whether there is a difference between the views of sūtra and mantra. When it comes to merely resolving the object of evaluation, meaning the basic space of phenomena free from constructs, the views of these two traditions are the same. However, there is a difference in the way that the subject sees the basic space of phenomena. Since the view is set forth from the perspective of the subject, this difference is, in fact, immense. Still, if the object resolved through the view—the basic space of phenomena, or suchness—was not identical in sūtra and mantra, it would absurdly follow that all phenomena would have different types of suchness. Other absurd consequences would be that one could not perceive suchness through the sūtric path of seeing, and that reasoning would have to prove that there is further construction to be eliminated beyond the constructs of the four extremes.

Consequently, all the learned and accomplished masters are in agreement when it comes to this single essential point: reality is directly seen on the path of seeing in both sūtra and mantra. This may lead one to think that the superiority of the mantric view is untenable since the object of both views is the same. Nevertheless, the superiority of the mantric view is, indeed, tenable.

> Although their purport is identical,
> The vehicle of mantra is exceedingly sublime,
> As it is undeluded, rich in means, without hardship,
> And meant for those with sharp faculties.

As alluded to here, the mantric vehicle is superior in two ways: (1) it employs knowledge to bring about a distinct freedom from delusion and (2) with its distinctive abundance of skillful methods, it allows one to behold the natural state in a swift manner. Therefore, as a path, it is both convenient and swift. Hence, it involves no hardships. As for the individual, or support, who is fit for this vehicle, mantra is the domain of those with sharper faculties than those who are influenced exclusively by the causal vehicle. In this way, mantra is exceedingly sublime.

When someone with excellent vision and someone else with impaired vision look at the same figure from far away, we can distinguish between accurate and distorted perception. In the same way, mantra is superior to sūtra, both in terms of the way one attains vivid experience during meditative equipoise and also how one gains certainty during the ensuing attainment.

Concerning the first, at the beginning of the path of sūtra, one uses inference to meditate intellectually on the basic space of phenomena. In addition, one also gathers the accumulations on a vast scale. In this way, the basic space of phenomena is realized in actuality after an extended duration. In mantra, however, one is able to realize the basic space of phenomena within the nature of one's own mind. This realization, moreover, is a direct experience and utterly free of any speculation. Here one attains a vivid experience of the natural state through the power of the ripening empowerments and the extraordinary vital points of the key instructions.

This is similar to clearly seeing a distant figure after applying ointment to one's eyes, or undoing the secret rope by becoming skilled in the essential points of incisive yogic exercises. Moreover, even though the key point of intellectual meditation on the path of sūtra does ultimately come down to the inseparability of the two truths, it is difficult for a beginner to ascertain, or experience, the equal taste of the unity of the two truths. Therefore, such individuals primarily grasp at emptiness as being a negation of individual extremes. In mantra, however, the unified wisdom of luminosity is revealed in its natural state. On this point, the *Wheel of Time* explains:

> Unlike what the realists believe, *the three existences are not* established as *forms* consisting *of minute* particles or consciousness. Rather, what exists *here is* merely *consciousness* free from apprehended or apprehender. This is the assertion of the Mind Only School. However, if one investigates this claim, *as is the case with* the smallest particle, even *consciousness* itself *does not* truly *exist*. "*The insight of the Buddha was that no phenomena dwells anywhere.* That is the Middle Way." *These words taught by Buddhists lack* the unchanging bliss. *People* who lack this *merely apprehend emptiness. In this way, they view the empty* and are unable to give up reference points. *Therefore*, in the "Wheel of Time" *the Lord has taught the vehicle of mantra to be an unchanging and innate physical bliss* that dwells in the body, yet does not arise from it.

In this way, mantra is superior to sūtra in terms of the vivid experience of meditative equipoise and the naked experience of the meaning of the unity of bliss and emptiness, or of basic space and awareness.

Secondly, when one experiences this unity of bliss and emptiness, or the unity of basic space and awareness, the naturally pure expanse is spontaneously present. This expanse is suchness, the natural state of all phenomena, and it is spontaneously present within the aspect of awareness as the bodies and wisdoms, which are beyond meeting and parting in essence. The natural state is the unity of appearance and emptiness; there are no impure appearances in this natural state. Therefore, within the natural state of luminosity, the bodies and wisdoms are self-display. Their divisions display innumerable qualities of enlightenment, exceeding the number of grains of sand on the riverbed of the Ganges. This is not only the assertion of mantra, but also of the common great vehicle. In this regard, the *Supreme Continuity* states:

> Exceeding the number of grains of sand in the Ganges,
> Inconceivable, unequalled, and full of qualities—
> This pristine basic field of the thus-gone ones
> Is free from flaws and their habitual patterns.

This demonstrates that the basic space at the time of the completely pure fruition and the naturally present potential are essentially free of change and without any qualitative difference. Therefore, by attaining a vivid experience of reality during meditative equipoise, one will give rise to the supreme certainty that all apparent phenomena are none other than the expanse of great equality, reality itself. Moreover, one will also gain certainty in the primordially pure nature of all appearances, which neither meet nor part from equality. This extraordinary certainty of the subsequent attainment is the view of secret mantra.

Seeing the luminous basic space, exactly as it is, is to attain the wisdom of the sūtra path of seeing. Through this, during meditative equipoise one sees the meaning of the great equality of the basic space of phenomena, in a way that is beyond subject-object duality. Such perception is without concepts, such as pure/impure and existent/nonexistent. By virtue of having seen the basic space of phenomena in actuality, one then realizes the meaning of great purity and equality exactly as it is. This realization takes place within a state of ascertainment during the ensuing attainment. The *Supreme Continuity* explains:

> Since the nature of mind is luminous, they see disturbing emotions
>   to be without essence.

> Thereby, they genuinely realize all beings to be selfless, pacified of extremes;
> They possess the stainless intelligence—seeing that the perfect buddha permeates all.
> I bow to the ones who are endowed with the wisdom that sees the complete purity of the infinite number of sentient beings.

It should go without saying that one will not become enlightened unless one realizes this meaning of great equality and purity on the path of mantra, in which cause and effect are inseparable. One will not even be able to see the truth of the intrinsic nature in an accurate manner!

One may argue that because all that appears and exists is not taught to be great purity, the nature of primordial enlightenment, on the path of sūtra, it is impossible to see the truth through the path of sūtra alone. On the path of sūtra, one gathers the accumulations and grows accustomed to the significance of the teaching that shows all phenomena to be equality, and does so for one incalculable eon. After an extended duration, this is capable of naturally inducing the ascertainment of the great purity of appearance and existence, the significance of which had hitherto remained hidden on one's path. On the three pure grounds, for instance, the universe and its inhabitants are seen as pure and one realizes the equality of existence and peace. The practice of these pure grounds—both the equality of existence and peace and the establishment of pure realms—is the actualization of purity and equality as explained in mantra. Hence, by applying skillful methods, it is as though one is able to actualize independently the means of mantra by which one swiftly becomes enlightened. Not only that, according to the sūtras, one can become enlightened in a week, if one so wishes, once the first ground is attained.

Thus, there are two options. One either becomes enlightened swiftly through mantra or gains realization of the meaning taught in mantra after an extended period of time. However, one should know that these two come down to the same essential point; there is no contradiction in terms of their intent. A great deal more can be said on this topic, but we shall leave the discussion for now as these issues are addressed elsewhere.

The causal vehicle of characteristics is referred to as such because it asserts that, while all phenomena are a great equality in the ultimate sense, in terms of the relative, cause and effect and accepting and rejecting are different and, moreover, saṃsāra is not enlightened in and of itself. Such beliefs create delusion concerning the fact that all phenomena are enlightened.

In contrast, on the path of mantra, one views saṃsāra and nirvāṇa as an indivisible great purity from the very beginning, even while eliminating misconceptions through study and contemplation. Therefore, the view is free from delusion; the truth of origin arises as the essence of the truth of the path, and the truth of suffering as the essence of the truth of cessation. In this way, afflictive emotions are liberated as wisdoms and suffering as great bliss. Hence, this approach is referred to as the "fruitional vehicle" and the "vajra vehicle" because effects are seen to be inseparable from their causes. For these same reasons, the aggregates, elements, and sense sources are explained using the term "vajra."

2. The View of Mantra
This section has two parts: a proof of the view's individual elements and a proof of the view in general.

1. Individual Elements of the View
This explanation proves purity, equality, and inseparability.

1. Purity
This section proves the principle of purity and disposes of claims that this principle is untenable.

1. The Principle of Purity
The explanation of this principle involves proving (1) appearances to be divine and (2) the subject to be wisdom.

1. The Divinity of Appearances
This section consists of the actual proof of purity via the valid cognition that investigates the conventional and proof by the force of the valid cognition that investigates the ultimate.

1. Conventional Valid Cognition
There are a number of ways to prove the divinity of appearance in a way that accords with the experience of those who accept the existence of external

objects. Here, however, I will simply offer an explanation of the essential points of this argument. The same body of water may appear to hungry ghosts as pus and blood, to humans as water, to those who dwell in pure realms as a stream of nectar, and to noble knowledge holders with pure vision as the form of Māmakī. Touching it performs the function of moistening and produces playful bliss and nonconceptual meditative absorption. For buddhas, who have completely exhausted all latent tendencies, nothing appears from the perspective of seeing things as they are, for all constructs without exception have been pacified. From the perspective of seeing things in their multiplicity, however, appearances are seen as complete purity, the embodiment of limitless self-displayed domains of wisdom activity.

At this point, one may wonder which of these ways of seeing is valid, and which object is established in accordance with conventional reality. The purer the subject, the more valid its cognition. What a given subject sees can be established to be the natural state. This is similar to objects, such as a white conch and yellow conch, and the minds that apprehend them. In this way, it follows that the natural state of all appearances can be proven to be the bodies and maṇḍalas of wisdom. The reason, here, is that their purity is perceived by noble beings who are free from distorting pollutants, just as a conch will be perceived to be white by someone with unimpaired vision.

Evidence of this can be established using both scripture and reasoning. First, let us consider scripture as evidence. It is generally acknowledged in scripture that those who have attained the wisdom of transformation, such as those who dwell on the pure grounds, experience pure realms and other forms of pure perception. In light of this fact, one may argue that the noble ones see a self-display, whereas that which is seen by ordinary beings is not seen as pure. If this were the case, however, it would absurdly follow that there are no objects of perception that can be shared by both pure and impure beings. This, however, is not the case.

Take the case of Śāriputra, who saw the Buddha's realm as impure, and Brahmaśikhin, who saw it as pure. When they disputed, the Buddha made the pure realm visible to everybody and said: "Although my realm is always pure like this, you do not see it." If authentic perception and mistaken perception were unable to evaluate the nature of the same object, then whatever is seen by anyone would become valid cognition. In this way, one would be unable to tell the difference between the truth and falsity of the appearance of a yellow and white conch, respectively. Consequently, were any tradition to propose such a theory, all categories of validity and invalidity would vanish.

Therefore, apart from pure self-display, there are no impure objects. The *Condensed Sūtra of Transcendent Knowledge* states:

> The purity of form should be known as the purity of fruition.
> Pure fruition and form are pure in omniscience.
> In omniscience, the purity of the fruition and the purity of form
> Are equal like the element of space—indivisible and inseparable.

Objects are seen in a pure manner when the subject is purified of stains. In this way, the precise nature of the object becomes evident, like the perception that overturns the apprehension of a conch being yellow.

Second, let us consider evidence established through reasoning. The fact that the same object can be perceived in different ways is something that is clearly accepted and proven in this world, and if one has become accustomed to all phenomena being indivisible from the naturally pure basic space, one will only perceive appearances that are characterized by natural purity. This occurrence of consummate vivid appearance can be established through inference.

The basic argument is sound because as pure seeing is unmistaken, whatever is seen in that mode must necessarily be in accordance with fact. If this were not so, pure seeing would have to be false and impure seeing would prove to be true. In that case, we would have to assert that the noble ones perceive erroneously and ordinary beings perceive correctly. What respectful and reasonable individuals would ever make such a claim?

In this way, the higher forms of perception refute lower ones, while lower ones do not invalidate higher ones. On this point, *Entering the Middle Way* states:

> The observation of someone with an eye-disorder
> Does not invalidate the cognition of one with healthy eyes.
> Likewise, a mind that lacks stainless wisdom
> Cannot invalidate a stainless mind.

Buddhas, who have completely purified all stains, see all that exists and, from this perspective, see all phenomena in a pure manner. Since this perception cannot be superseded, it is established as the final conventional mode of relative phenomena. In this way, it is of the utmost importance to understand that all these relative phenomena have two modes: the way they appear to confused perception and the natural state of the relative itself.

To believe that valid cognition that investigates the conventional is nothing but the confined perception of ordinary people, and that what is seen by that confined vision alone is the final natural state of the conventional is extremely closed-minded. When examined carefully, only a coarse intellect would see no reason to differentiate between the perception that a conch is white and the perception that a conch is yellow as, respectively, valid and invalid cognitions. If the natural state of any given entity were nothing more than the way it appears to an ordinary being, then the appearance of a yellow conch to the one who perceives it as such would also be the conch's true natural state.

One may think, "But such perception is distorted, insofar as it is caused by delusion; it is not a perception of the natural state." Nevertheless, even though these impure appearances that are tainted by erroneous habitual conditioning are perceivable by ordinary people, one must assert that their natural state is the way they appear to pure beings, which are free from such stains. Therefore, to give a brief account of this extremely profound key point, we will discuss the thoroughly conventional valid cognitions. There are two such valid cognitions: the thoroughly conventional valid cognition based on confined vision and the thoroughly conventional valid cognition based on pure vision. In brief, the difference between these two can be explained in terms of their cause, essence, function, and result.

The valid cognition of confined vision is caused by a correct examination of its particular, limited object. In essence, it is a temporarily undeceiving awareness of merely its specific object. It functions to eliminate superimpositions regarding the objects of confined vision. It results in an engagement based on having fully determined the object at hand.

The valid cognition of pure seeing is caused by having correctly observed reality as it truly is. In essence, it is a vast knowledge concerning all possible subjects. It functions to eliminate superimpositions concerning a field of experience that the confined perception of ordinary beings cannot fathom. It results in the accomplishment of the wisdom that knows all there is.

These two valid cognitions can be likened to the human eye and the divine eye, respectively. The valid cognition of pure vision knows the object of confined vision, yet confined vision does not know the objects of the valid cognition of pure vision. The object of the latter is, therefore, unique. Instances of this are the appearance of as many buddha-fields as there are dust motes in the world in a single dust mote, performing activities of many eons in a single moment, displaying emanations while not departing from the unchanging basic space of phenomena, and knowing all objects of cognition in a single instant with a nonconceptual mind.

These inconceivable experiences appear to conflict with the objects of ordinary confined vision. For this reason, this form of perception cannot be used to prove them. Yet this valid cognition can prove all of them as perfectly reasonable. The valid cognition of completely pure wisdom manifests by force of the reasoning of the inconceivable natural state. Therefore, it is extremely powerful, never deceptive, supramundane, pure, unexcelled, and unequaled.

All that can be commonly proven through the path of confined perception, such as proving the authenticity of our teacher, is established using the valid cognition of confined vision. The unique inconceivable experiences of the thus-gone ones, in contrast, are proven with the valid cognition of pure vision by being in accord with the natural state. In this way, one should be knowledgeable concerning the essential point that profound principles, such as the primordial enlightenment of all phenomena, are not proven exclusively by means of confined perception, yet neither are they utterly without a valid means of proof.

Without knowing this, one will be unable to draw any qualitative distinctions between nonattached non-Buddhists and the four sublime ones with respect to their ability to perceive sentient beings within the mere width of a chariot wheel, nor will one be able to note the difference between an erroneous cognition that grows increasingly mistaken and a view that becomes increasingly sublime. There will also be no qualitative distinction made between the degree of knowledge possessed by those with different status, like the Buddha seeing the seed of liberation in the being of the householder Śrīsambhava, while the foe destroyers did not. In this way, one will not gain conviction in teachings, such as the following passage from a sūtra:

> Even upon the tip of one hair
> There are an inconceivable number of buddha-fields.
> Their various shapes are all distinct;
> They are clearly separate.

This issue is, therefore, of great import in both sūtra and mantra.

2. Purity and Ultimate Valid Cognition
The term "impure" refers to nothing more than the appearances that comprise the truths of suffering and its origin. The appearances that dwell in unity with basic space, which is empty of the two selves, can be established as neither the essence nor the object of disturbing emotions, such as grasping at a self, nor can they be established as the identity of the karma and suffering that are produced by the disturbing emotions. Therefore, not even the names of the impurities contained within the truths of suffering and its origin exist. Everything dwells naturally in a state of purity.

Therefore, since there is no phenomenon that is not of the nature of the great equality of emptiness, all of appearance and existence is proven to be primordial great purity. The principle of purity is not simply expressed from the perspective of emptiness, in which no phenomena exist. Rather, because appearances themselves are inseparable from emptiness, they are shown to be great bliss, exactly in the way they appear. They are always sublime and primordially pure.

2. The Subject as Wisdom
Great purity can be proven in the following way to philosophers who do not accept any shared external object of perception, and who instead assert that all phenomena are merely the mind's own display. First there is an occasion of impurity, in which various appearances of the six classes are perceived. As the mind conceives in various dualistic ways, they appear through the fully developed force of solidifying habitual patterns. Pure appearances manifest in the context of the path free from error, while the boundless appearances of complete purity manifest in the context of the fruition, at which point the entire range of obscurations have been exhausted.

All of these appearances are none other than the self-display of one's own mind. While functioning as the basis for all of them, however, the mind is luminous and empty of the two selves. It dwells as the unobstructed manifestation of various appearances. When the mind's apprehensions are out of touch with the way things are, it apprehends a self, as well as subject and object, thereby producing disturbing emotions that, in turn, create karma. As a result of this, all the various appearances that are subsumed under the truth of suffering can manifest, just like appearances in a dream. All of these confused experiences are not grounded in reality; they are unreliable and deceptive.

By training on the path in accordance with the mind's natural state, the confused aspect of self-display will gradually be reversed. When this happens, pure appearances will faultlessly dawn and will no longer revert back. As these appearances are undeceiving and in tune with reality, they appear faultlessly as mere conventional self-display. Thus, confused appearances are not true, while pure appearances are true, insofar as they are free of stains.

For instance, if one blends the element of gold that comes from earth and metal with the likes of the finest gold and the element of quicksilver, which comes from coal, water, and herbal ingredients, it will come to resemble a single mass, like a glob of fresh butter. As the object of sense-faculties like the eye, these ingredients will not be evident, while one may still understand it to possess various ingredients as an object of the mind. Confused individuals will perceive it to be a mass of butter or grease. Others will see it as a cause of gold, with the mere understanding that it will become gold once burned. Learned individuals, on the other hand, will see that it possesses various constituents and will perceive its ability to appear in various ways depending upon the various conditions it meets with. When such a mass is cold, it will remain like a mass of fresh butter for an extremely long time. When it touches a flame and heats up, however, it will become the color of copper, bronze, and brass. Likewise, when heated with a strong flame, it will become the nature of ordinary gold, and will become the nature of the finest gold when heated thoroughly. From that point on, it will not change in nature, no matter what temperature its surroundings are.

The all-ground consciousness can be understood in a similar fashion. The all-ground, the container of all seeds, manifests as the entire range of appearances. In the same way that a mass can appear differently to those of various faculties, the all-ground may appear in specific contexts as environs, bodies, and objective experiences that are either pure, impure, or completely pure. Just as one may understand the mass to possess various ingredients, the mental consciousness realizes that the seeds for an infinite range of appearances throughout time and space are present within the all-ground, regardless of whether or not they have actually manifested from the all-ground.

In the same way that the mass may be confused for a chunk of butter, some may apprehend all the appearances of the all-ground as a self and phenomena. Moreover, just as some may perceive the mass as quicksilver, some people apprehend the aggregates as suffering, being characterized by the ripening of karma. Similar to apprehending the mass to be the cause of gold, some perceive the aggregates themselves as the cause for the completely pure bodies and experiences of those who live in the pure realms. Learned individuals understand that, although the mass itself is not gold, it is not without the nature of gold either. Although it appears to be quicksilver, it is not the case that the gold transformed into quicksilver, nor is it the case that it lacks the nature of quicksilver. Such individuals will say that the nature of quicksilver is unstable and that it is easy for it to transform into a variety of things. They know that the nature of gold is much more stable, for it is difficult to transform and will not diminish in quality. Even when burned in a blazing fire, it will not be readily depleted.

Likewise, impure phenomena are unstable and extremely deceptive. The appearances of past and future lives are mutable and exhausted by cultivating the path. Pure appearances, however, are the exact opposite. As soon as one has mastered a pure body and experience, one will never have to experience impurity again. One will develop supreme bliss, which is completely pure and free from suffering. In this way, pure appearances are reliable and undeceiving.

Therefore, when compared with other perceptions, the mass with various constituents will truly become the nature of gold. Likewise, the all-ground, endowed as it is with various potentials and appearances, truly is the domain of pure appearances. When all the temporary habitual patterns related to delusion have run out, they will produce no more appearances. Nevertheless, the spontaneously present appearances of unobstructed natural radiance that occur within primordial basic space cannot possibly be retracted since they are essentially inseparable from it. Therefore, pure self-displays of stainless wisdom are pure in actuality.

In this way, if the identity of all saṃsāric phenomena is proven to be the pure deity, one may wonder what this term actually means. The actual deity of reality itself is the wisdom of nondual appearance and emptiness. It is the vajra body free from the obscurations of transference. It is the enlightenment of equal taste, where even the most subtle habitual tendency to obscure the reality of suchness has run out. It is inconceivable, free from the confines of singularity and multiplicity. Although beyond the entire realm of characteristics, it manifests in the form of all that can be known. It is the body of self-occurring wisdom, which is without difference and distinction from all the bliss-gone ones of the three times. It is enlightenment as the equality of all of saṃsāra and nirvāṇa. This is the ultimate deity, the universal master of all buddha families.

The subject, the symbolic deity, manifests in the symbolic form of the wisdom body itself, which transcends the domain of signs. As taught in each individual tantra, they appear in peaceful and wrathful forms with attributes like faces and hands, as main deities and their retinues, and as the support and supported.

Therefore, since all phenomena are of the same character within the expanse of the equality of appearance and emptiness, they are pure in being the essence of the main deity within the maṇḍala of the one with the body of vajra wisdom. Alternatively, since body, speech, and mind are the three vajras in nature, they are pure in being the three buddha families, while the five aggregates are pure as the five buddha families. In this way, phenomena can be classified into five or one hundred buddha families, all the way up to the inconceivable families of the magical net. The rationale here is that one can make as many divisions of purity as there are appearances of impurity, and that there is not even a single phenomenon whose essence wavers from the natural state of great purity and equality.

Reality is nothing whatsoever, yet from it, anything can arise. Due to this key point, its self-display manifests impartially and without limitation as the display of the magical net. Therefore, while the innumerable buddhas and their buddha-fields are completely pure, any amount of classification can be accommodated, no matter what distinctions are being made. The reason is that no phenomenon is beyond the identity of self-occurring wisdom, great purity and equality, the reality beyond one and many. Hence, purity is contextualized in various ways in the various classes of tantra, according to the enumeration of their respective deities. The *Tantra of the Secret Essence* also teaches the principle of great purity in the following lines:

> The world, beings, and continua are realized to be pure.

And:

> The secret bindu is the basic space of the maṇḍala.
> The elements are knowledge, the mother of the families.
> The great ones are the suchness of the families.

> The awakened mind is the vajra assembly,
> As are the faculties, objects, time, and awareness,
> Seen in the maṇḍala of Samantabhadra
> By the five wisdoms of the enlightened mind
> Of the superior illustrious being.

Other tantras teach this as well. The *Hevajra Tantra*, for instance, explains:

> Sentient beings are actual buddhas,
> Yet obscured by temporary stains.

While the *Wheel of Time* states:

> Sentient beings are buddhas.
> There are no other illustrious buddhas in this world.

In the *Conduct Tantra of the Yoginī*, it is said:

> The identity of all these beings is that of the five buddhas.
> They appear just like dancers or superb paintings.
> That which is called "great bliss" is singularity,
> Manifesting dances of plurality within the experience of singularity.

And the *Heruka Galpo* states:

> Through the causal vehicle of characteristics,
> Sentient beings are understood to be the cause of buddhas.
> Yet the fruitional vehicle of mantra
> Meditates on mind itself as buddha.

Furthermore, according to the common great vehicle, it is also taught that all phenomena are in all ways fully and truly enlightened.

2. Relinquishing the Untenability of Purity

This section contains both a general and a specific way to refute critiques of purity. First, concerning the general refutation, some narrow-minded individuals may object that meditating on the world and its inhabitants on the path may merely cause them to *appear* to be pure, although this is not actually the case. The reason given is that while they may appear in this manner, their nature is of the truths of suffering and its origin.

We also accept that those of us with impure minds and impure eyes perceive things in an impure manner. Nonetheless, if everyone experienced pure appearances, what would there be to argue about? Although things may appear in an impure manner, this is not how they actually are. In fact, in their natural state, they are naturally pure. If one makes such an assertion, appearances do not necessarily have to appear the way they truly are because they can appear incorrectly to a mind tainted by confusion. This is no different than an eye cognition that perceives a snow mountain to be blue.

This is explained in the *Root Knowledge of the Middle Way*:

> If an objection is made through emptiness,
> Whatever may be replied
> Will not be a reply,
> But the same as what is yet to be proven.

For instance, when resolving all phenomena to be empty, no matter what phenomenon is posited to prove that things are not empty—including the causality of karma, saṃsāra, and nirvāṇa—the proof will amount to the same as what is still to be proven, and so one can prove that also the proof itself lacks inherent existence. Hence, whatever is set forth to prove that things are not empty becomes an aid to the reasoning that establishes emptiness, just like adding fuel to fire. Just as one will be unable to find a reasoning that disproves emptiness, any proof that is put forward to establish that phenomena are impure will itself be shown to be purity. Therefore, no matter where one searches, one will not succeed in finding an argument that can disprove the reasoning that establishes all phenomena to be pure in their natural state.

> When using great purity in an argument,
> Whatever may be replied
> Will not be a reply,
> But the same as what is yet to be proven.

Furthermore, if sentient beings are buddhas, would it not follow that buddhas suffer when sentient beings are miserable in hell? The answer is no. The misery in hell is merely apparent to the confused perception of those who have not realized the natural state. From the perspective of the way things appear, they are not buddhas. Therefore, this objection does not hold. There is no such thing as suffering in the natural state. The *Elaborate Magical Net* says:

> Without the self-awareness of authentic knowing,
> Even the realms of the bliss-gone ones are seen as the lower realms.
> If one realizes the meaning of the equality of the supreme vehicle,
> These hellish abodes themselves are the abodes of the unexcelled
>   and joyous.

Some may infer other absurd consequences as well, such as saying that if all phenomena are primordially enlightened by their very nature, they should be universally perceived as such and there would be no need for cultivating the path. This attitude is pitifully small-minded. Claiming this would be tantamount to saying that a white conch should be perceived as such by even a visually impaired individual, and that there would be no need to try to heal such an impairment.

Therefore, when things do not appear the way they truly are, it is because the stains of confusion cause this to happen. Hence the path must be cultivated to counter confusion. Although the nature of all phenomena is emptiness, one must practice the path for it to be actualized.

Consequently, any attempt to refute great equality is dispensed with in a way similar to the response to refutations of emptiness. When applying reasoning, both purity and equality are mutually confirming and of a single key point. Since both are the nature of things, the proof of great purity is an extremely forceful reasoning arrived at through the power of fact. As such, it reigns supreme and cannot be invalidated.

Second, concerning the specific refutation, some may object that, even though purity can be proven in this way, if a buddha's wisdom only sees everything as pure, the objects and subjects appearing to the perception of confused beings will not be observed. Consequently, if they were not seen, a buddha would not be omniscient. Yet if they were, a buddha would see impure phenomena.

The wisdom of omniscience allows buddhas to know appearances in the way they appear, even those that appear to be impure. Still, it is not that these impure appearances truly exist, or that buddhas perceive phenomena that are proven to be impure. Buddhas see clearly how objects seem to be true to those who cling to true existence, likewise they see how the subject fixates on their true existence. Nevertheless, a buddha will not view any phenomenon as truly existent because it is impossible for such a being to see even the tiniest particle as truly established. In this way, since buddhas perceive all phenomena as a self-display, it can be proven that buddhas only perceive purity.

2. Equality
This topic has two subdivisions: arguments that prove equality and how to gain certainty about this principle.

1. Arguments for Equality
If the phenomena of saṃsāra and nirvāṇa are properly examined with the logical arguments of the Middle Way, such as the one from lack of one and many, one will gain certainty that not even a subtle particle of any given entity is truly established. This holds not only for the impure phenomena of saṃsāra, but also the pure bodies and wisdoms.

2. Gaining Certainty about Equality
There may be people of sharp faculties who will analyze the mind in terms of its arising, abiding, and cessation, and thereby come to experience the nature of the three gates of liberation: emptiness of cause, effect, and essence. This alone will lead to an instantaneous certainty in the meaning of the equality of appearance and emptiness.

However, in terms of ascertaining equality in a gradual way, beginners should begin by correctly examining the reasons that prove emptiness, such as the logical analysis of investigating singularity and multiplicity. When one reflects on the meaning of nonexistence at that time, in relation to a vase, for instance, one will find that although things seem to exist when not investigated, nothing can be found upon analysis. Thereby, one will come to believe that nonexistence itself is the natural state. Thus, an image of emptiness manifests in a process of alternation between appearance and emptiness.

When at that time one reflects on the way that this nonexistence of phenomena is also just a mere imputation and not actually established, or on the way things appear while being primordially empty, one will develop an extraordinary certainty about phenomena being empty while apparent, and apparent while empty, like the moon's reflection in a pool of water. At that time, the absence of nature and dependent arising will dawn in a noncontradictory manner. This is referred to as "the understanding of unity." Although "absence of nature" and "dependent origination" are different expressions, here one gains certainty that these two are essentially inseparable and without the slightest difference.

Through this, the conceptual thought that connects appearance, the basis for negation, with an eliminated object of negation naturally falls away. In this way, the characteristics of freedom from constructs, such as the ability to remain naturally without negation and affirmation, adding and removing, will dawn. As one grows increasingly familiar with this freedom from constructs, the entirety of dualistic phenomena, in which a confined mind observes particular intrinsic natures in relation to individual subjects, becomes purified. This process reaches a point of culmination by bringing forth a distinctive certainty that the nature of all phenomena is one of equality.

In this way, one first understands emptiness, then unity, freedom from constructs, and, finally, equality. By understanding the former one gains access to the latter. However, until one has gained certainty in a preceding principle, one will not be able to resolve the subsequent stage. Submitting oneself to the idea that the categorized ultimate, the mere lack of true existence, is the natural state will not bring one even close to the equality that is demonstrated in this context.

Merely understanding the contradistinction that is the elimination of true existence, thinking this exists with reference to pillars, vases, and other such things, will not perform the function of equality, which is to do away with all notions of phenomena bearing marks and having good and bad qualities. Just so, a commoner cannot perform the duties of a king. Therefore, when perfecting the Middle Way path free from all constructs, all phenomena are seen to be equality. This is the realization of great equality referred to in this context. On this point, the *Tantra of the Secret Essence* says:

> Not understanding freedom from reference points,
> You do not comprehend the basic space of phenomena.
> Therefore, destroy entities and nonentities
> And thus apprehend freedom from reference points!

And also:

> Through the two equalities and the two superior equalities,
> There is the realm of the Samantabhadra maṇḍala.

Not only do the tantras teach this, but the common vehicle as well. For instance, the *Sūtra Requested by Kāśyapa* mentions:

> Kāśyapa, realizing all phenomena to be equality is nirvāṇa. This is one, not two and not three.

This explanation also demonstrates that ultimately there is only one vehicle. The *Sūtra That Shows the Way to Awakening* explains:

> Mañjuśrī, whoever sees that all phenomena are equal, nondual, and inseparable possesses the authentic view.

3. Inseparability

Purity is established from the perspective of appearance, and equality from the perspective of emptiness. Since these two are inseparable and of one taste within all phenomena, the inseparability of purity and equality is proven indirectly through each of these principles. Whatever appears in a pure manner is empty of all extremes; and whatever is equality, meaning free from all extremes, manifests as the extreme purity of the manifold appearances of the magical net. These two are inseparable within the single sphere of the dharma body. This is what the individual self-awareness of the sacred ones realizes and this is the manner of the great perfection of unity. On this point, the *Tantra of the Secret Essence* states:

> In the secret bindu, the basic space of suchness,
> Is the actuality of all the buddhas.
> One sees the very face of the embodiment of enlightened body,
> Speech, qualities, activities, and mind, without exception,
> Of the completely perfect ones in the ten directions and four times.
> This mastery is the most sacred and supreme.

And:

Self-occurring wisdom appears without abiding.

As for the way to practice this, it is said:

> Emptiness, the absence of self, is primordially known by self-awareness, the enlightened mind.
> With nothing to observe and nothing observing, mindfulness brings mastery.
> The amazing enlightened body, speech, qualities, and buddha fields,
> Are nowhere else; rather, it itself is just like this.

The *Compendium of Vajra Wisdom* states:

> Were the two truths separate,
> The path of wisdom would be pointless.
> If clarity and emptiness were separate,
> One would fall into the extremes of eternalism and nihilism.

And:

> Since the essence of all phenomena is beyond a path,
> By perfecting it you are freed from effort and strain.
> The completely pure innate wisdom,
> Is a nonabiding unity.

The *Nondual Victory* likewise explains:

> Since they are profound, vast and inseparable,
> Appearance and emptiness are inseparably mixed.
> This is taught to be the buddha
> And demonstrates the principle of enlightenment.

While the *Vajra Garland Tantra* states:

> The relative and the ultimate,
> When free of these two concepts,
> They are completely integrated.
> This is explained to be "unity."

2. General Explanations
This explanation has two subdivisions: establishing the present meaning directly to fortunate individuals and indirectly to skeptics.

1. Directly Establishing the Meaning
The meaning of the inseparability of purity and equality, which is beyond the intellect, is established by means of four realizations:
1) In the equality of the basic space of phenomena, all phenomena are established to be of a single cause, or a single mode.
2) The apparent aspect of this equality is the wisdoms and bodies. These are established through the principle of the seed syllable, as various syllables can manifest from certain conditions, such as the single sound of the syllable "A."
3) The single cause and the principle of syllables mutually bless each other and are beyond meeting and parting.
4) In this way, the meaning of the great dharma body, the inseparability of purity and equality, is experienced through one's own self-awareness in a way that transcends the intellect.

As an alternative to this gradual explanation:
1) In the essence of the inseparability of the truths of purity and equality, all phenomena are of a single taste and a single cause.
2) This is exemplified by the syllable OṂ, which is illustrated by the three syllables A, U and M. These three, in turn, demonstrate the inseparable nature of enlightened body, speech, and mind, and of the three gates to complete liberation.
3) By the force, or blessing, of these two arguments of meaning and metaphor, all phenomena are resolved to be primordially enlightened as great purity and equality.
4) Although this meaning can be proven to be in accord with scripture and key instructions, it is not resolved through speculations that merely rely on the words of the scriptures and key instructions. The view of mantra is resolved from the depth of one's heart through the four direct ways of gaining certainty.

Here, unity is pointed out from the very beginning, so explanation pertains to the instantaneous type. Still, in both cases, the four reasons, such as that of the single cause, are undeceiving means for accessing the profound view of mantra. Therefore, they are called "arguments."

2. Indirectly Establishing the Meaning

The meaning of the primordial enlightenment of all phenomena is extremely difficult to comprehend. For this reason, some individuals will find it implausible. To such people, one can explain the meaning indirectly in the following manner. First, while non-Buddhists are doubtful of the idea that Buddha is an authentic being, in the Vedic scriptures, which they themselves believe in, it is said:

> On occasions as rare as the occurrence of an udumbāra flower, an omniscient teacher appears in this world in the ruling or priestly caste. When entering the womb, his mother dreams that he enters in the form of an elephant. When born, he displays major and minor marks. If he does not renounce the world, he will become a universal monarch; if he does, he will become enlightened.

In this way, such scriptures establish the existence of the Buddha.

From a logical perspective, the path shown by the Buddha, such as the absence of personal self, can be proven to be a liberating path through the reasoning of the power of fact. Moreover, as this is the case, the Buddha can be proven to be an authentic teacher for anyone who seeks liberation, and the path that he taught can be proven to be authentic. In establishing our teacher's authenticity, the chapter "Establishing Validity" and other sources prove just this.

Though listeners believe in the existence of the Buddha, they do not believe in the emptiness taught in the great vehicle. As for scripture, however, their own lesser vehicle sūtras make statements such as "form is like a mass of foam." Moreover, from a logical point of view, if one fails to see the five aggregates' lack of true existence, insofar as they are composite and momentary, one will not establish the absence of personal self. Therefore, just as the *Jewel Garland* explains, it can be proven that liberation is accomplished based on emptiness.

There are also scriptural and logical defenses directed toward those followers of the sūtra path who do not believe in the profound view and conduct of secret mantra. In terms of scripture, the *Royal Sūtra of Bestowing Instructions* prophesizes the later appearance of mantra. Moreover, the *Sūtra of the Ornamental Array* explains the five aggregates to be of the nature of the thus-gone ones:

> Whoever dwells in the equal nature
> Of oneself and the buddhas,
> Does not abide or appropriate;
> He or she is a thus-gone one.
>
> Form, feeling, perception,
> Consciousness, and intention
> Are the countless thus-gone ones;
> They are the great sage.

The *Vimalakīrti Sūtra* says:

> Disturbing emotions are the lineage of the thus-gone ones.

And:

> The teaching that freedom from desire and other such factors is liberation is taught forh arrogant individuals; the liberation of selfless individuals is taught to be the nature of desire and other such factors.

Moreover, afflictive emotions themselves are taught to be wisdom in certain scriptures, such as the *Sūtra of Mañjuśrī's Display,* which says:

> Disturbing emotions are the vajra bases of awakening.

For instance, the *Sūtra of the Emanations of Mañjuśrī* says:

> Nirvāṇa is not something that is cultivated through abandoning saṃsāra. Instead, nirvāṇa is to observe saṃsāra itself.

This shows that saṃsāra is enlightenment. Also, the *Avataṃsakasūtra* states:

> Though numerous worlds may burn
> In the most inconceivable ways,
> Space will not disintegrate.
> Such is the case with self-occurring wisdom.

Citations such as this teach self-occurring wisdom. Moreover, the sūtras teach that all sentient beings possess the core of self-occurring wisdom. There are also countless statements that explain how, although Buddha Śākyamuni's realm is always pure, it is not seen as such. There are even statements in sūtras about pleasing the Buddha with a woman's body:

> A Bodhisattva should transform his own body into a female body in order to please the Thus-Gone One and then always remain before the Thus-Gone One.

There are also many statements that teach how to compassionately annihilate people, such as those who harm the dharma.

Regardless of whether the situation calls for scriptural citations, such as the one just mentioned, or logical analysis, all phenomena—as they appear—are naturally purity and equality. Therefore, they are not established as saṃsāra and nirvāṇa, good and evil, or in terms of rejection and acceptance. As was explained before, secret mantra is proven to be the supreme vehicle. It is certain that from the moment you accept emptiness, purity can also gradually be established.

Again, there may be some for whom most of the mantra explanations make sense, but for whom the meaning of the actionless great perfection seems unreasonable. On this issue, scripturally, the unsurpassable tantras teach that sentient beings are of the identity of enlightenment, and that the aggregates, elements, and other such factors are pure in the sense of being divine. These scriptures also prove how one does not truly need to rely on activities involving maṇḍalas, tormas, and so on. They also point out the wisdom in the fourth empowerment.

Reasoning establishes the world and its inhabitants to be a primordial purity and equality. Therefore, one does not need to accomplish these factors anew through the path. For people who have realized this in the core of their hearts, a regimen of effortful pursuits is proven to be a great obstacle to the path. Hence, it can easily be established how the practice of uncontrived naturalness allows one to attain mastery over the self-display of wisdom appearances.

In this way, subsequent points will not be established unless the points that precede them are proven as well. In teaching a sequence of vehicles that are like the rungs of a ladder, the Buddha showed how to cleanse the jewel of the basic potential. If one were to explain the profound secret to narrow-minded people who have yet to gain confidence in more basic topics, they will give it up or disparage it out of fear. Therefore, these instructions are extremely secret.

If, on the other hand, the profound realization of the view of the unsurpassable mantra is taught to those who have gained confidence in the meaning of great equality as explained in the sūtra vehicle, it will make sense to them. Therefore, being well versed in all the gradual vehicles will enable one to establish the final philosophy of the vajra pinnacle. Though endless when examined in detail, these explanations are meant to be a mere gateway into reasoning.

4. Purpose
The view serves both a both a general and a specific purpose.

1. General Purpose
While on the path, all practices are accessed according to one's own personal view. This is the nature of things. Thus, all practices of the vajra vehicle are exclusively practiced according to one's understanding of the principles of purity and equality. This view is like the capacity to see. Without it, awareness and "legs" will be missing as well. In this way, meditation and other such factors of the path will be a mere facade. On the other hand, any practice that is imbued with an authentic view such as this will become the true path of the vajra vehicle. As the key point of all paths comes down to this alone, it is of paramount importance.

2. Specific Purpose
Everything unfolds through the force of the view: meditation becomes unmistaken, conduct meaningful, the maṇḍala accords with reality, and the attainment comes through the bestowal of empowerment. Likewise, it

becomes difficult to transgress the samayas, the practice will not be squandered, offerings become completely pure, mastery is gained over enlightened activity, and mudrās and mantras become sublime.

If all phenomena were not purity and equality, meditating on the divine nature of the world and its inhabitants, the support and the supported, would be a form of training that conflicted with reality and one's meditation would be mistaken. However, since one is meditating on the way things are, this is not the case and the practice is not mistaken.

The same goes for conduct. If there is purity and equality, it is reasonable to engage in actions that accord with the view, such as the disciplined conduct of freely enjoying sense pleasures, being free from accepting and rejecting, and engaging in union and liberation. Were this not the case, it would be true that these are all to be abandoned, as is stated in the common vehicles, and engaging in them would be immoral. Therefore, it is due to the essential point of purity and equality that these mantric practices become meaningful.

Regarding the maṇḍala, the natural maṇḍala of the inseparable ground and fruition is represented by the symbolic maṇḍala and the maṇḍala of the path. The fruitional maṇḍala appears due to the path. However, if the ground were not like this, the path would not be authentic either, and no pure fruition could appear from it. By resolving the ground exactly as it is, the maṇḍala accords with reality.

As for empowerment, one's own body, speech, and mind, along with their equal aspects, dwell primordially as the four vajras. This is to be understood, experienced, and realized through the power of the empowerment, just like a vase seen with the help of a lamp or the moon pointed out by a finger. Apart from this nature, there is no meaning to be pointed out through the empowerment. Thus, the attainments derived from empowerment likewise depend on the view.

In terms of the samayas of mantra, it is said that one should not doubt the explanations that all phenomena are naturally pure as the deity, nor should one conceptualize equality, which lies beyond names and other such factors, by identifying it with characteristics. If all phenomena were not purity and equality, whoever perceived them to lack these qualities would be in accord with reality and, thus, would not be committing a root downfall of mantra. This would also not accord with teachings given in the context of the path of freedom from desire.

Moreover, the samayas of conduct, such as not mortifying the aggregates and joyfully accepting sense pleasures, samaya substances, and mudrās are in accord with purity and equality. Were this not the case, they would truly be as explained in the lower vehicles. It would, therefore, not make sense that one would commit a root downfall by abandoning something that ought to be rejected. Therefore, one would be free to transgress the pledges of mantra. However, due to the essential point that everything is pure and equal, the samayas should definitely not be transgressed by turning away from the view and the actions that are played out from that view. Consequently, the samayas are hard to transgress.

In practice, the deity is inseparable from the aggregates, elements, and sense sources. If this is their natural state, then it makes sense to actualize this state as it is by practicing the path. Were this not the case, however, it would be like trying to wash charcoal white or meditating that mind is matter... no matter how much one were to try, there would be no change. Since it would then become impossible to accomplish the deity's indivisibility, one's practice would be squandered. However, through the key point of purity and equality, practice is not wasted in this manner.

As for making offerings, the five types of meat, the five nectars and other substances that the world considers dirty are used as principal offerings in mantra. If they were actually impure, offering them to the deities would not be a viable option. Still, one may believe that blessing them with mantras and mūdras makes them pure. If this were the case, then it would make better sense to offer pure things and bless them with mantras and mūdras. What special purpose would there be in offering impure things? Therefore, although it is fine to practice cleanliness as taught in action tantra, in this context the five nectars and other substances should be utilized to dismantle the notions of pure/impure and acceptance/rejection. Since these substances also manifest through the key point of natural purity and equality, they are completely pure as offerings.

Regarding enlightened activity, according to inner mantra one imagines oneself to be primordially indivisible from the enlightened body, speech, and mind of the thus-gone ones, and one practices specific activities thereby. These activities become supremely powerful, matching the enlightened deeds of the thus-gone ones. If one were not essentially divine from the beginning, mentally fabricating something that does not accord with reality would not accomplish anything of superior value. However, since everyone is of the nature of great purity and equality, we are all inseparable from the deity in reality. Since the practices of inner mantra are superior to the approach of action tantra and other systems, one is able to gain mastery over the activities of enlightenment.

Mantra and mūdra are more powerful than the locks and recitations of outer mantra. This superiority is due to the force of maintaining the practice of habituating oneself to the realization of one's own indivisibility from the deity. If they did not accord with reality, then reciting mantras and performing mudrās as outlined in the inner mantras would not by nature hold greater blessings than reciting the Buddha's dhāraṇī. However, the mantras and mūdras that are connected to the development and completion stages of unsurpassable mantra possess the perfect power of great blessings, for they are accomplished through the ability to unerringly engage with the meaning of great purity and equality.

Therefore, as the actual nature of things, great purity and equality are the objects one must resolve through the view. This key point establishes the meditations and other practices of mantra to be of an unmistaken nature and constituting a delightful and swift path. Through the view that realizes the meaning of purity and equality, one arrives at supreme confidence in all paths of mantra. With this confidence, all paths embraced by this view become authentic paths of mantra.

This concludes the brief explanation of the view of perfect knowledge, the first parameter in secret mantra.

2. Absorption

Absorption will be presented in terms of its (1) essence, (2) divisions, (3) practice, and (4) purpose.

1. Essence

> Whoever tames the crazed elephant of the mind
> By placing it in equanimity
> And fully relies on mantra and mudrā
> Will reap a great and wonderful spiritual attainment.

As this verse explains, the Sanskrit word *samādhi* means a balanced mind. It means to train the mind such that one is able to rest one-pointedly on an observed object. It can also mean to rest in accordance with, or in the same manner as, an object undisturbed by dullness, agitation, and other such factors.

2. Divisions
This topic has two divisions: (1) essential divisions and (2) temporal divisions.

1. Essential Divisions
The essential division concerns the absorptions of development and completion. Development stage meditation has four divisions, each of which purifies the predispositions related to one of the four types of birth. The elaborate version consists of making others one's own children, becoming the child of others, developing the five manifestations of enlightenment, and developing the fourfold vajra ritual. The medium-length version makes use of a threefold development ritual. In the condensed version, which is employed in anuyoga, the mere recitation of mantra triggers the visualization. In the extremely condensed version, as found in atiyoga, one completes the process of development in an instant of recollection.

Alternatively, in conformity with womb birth and miraculous birth, a dual division of the development stage into gradual and instantaneous approaches is also taught. Moreover, there is also a fivefold distinction that follows the five gradual practices, such as that of great emptiness. There are, in fact, a great number of other divisions, such as the absorptions that observe the meaning of the four seals of enlightened body, speech, mind, and activity. In actuality, however, all practices that are classified as development stage are termed "development stage absorptions."

The completion stage consists of the path of means and the path of liberation. The former may rely upon the upper and lower gates, while the latter consists of the gradual and instantaneous nonconceptual practices of unity.

2. Temporal Divisions
Absorption can be divided temporally into blessed practice, imputed practice, and perfect practice. The ultimate deity is indivisible basic space and wisdom. Through its power, the symbolic deity of the form body appears. If one visualizes such a deity, one's own essential nature will be blessed by the essential nature of the deity.

First, as one meditates on the deity, one trains devotedly with the knowledge that this process is like pouring an alchemical elixir on iron. Second, one trains to become competent with the understanding that the form body is produced from the pure awakened mind, just as one creates a statue from melted gold. Third, a practitioner who has realized his or her nature to be pure perfects the absorption instantaneously, just like a reflection clearly appearing in a limpid pond.

As the *Magical Net of Vairocana* mentions, these three trainings embody, not only the entirety of mantra, but also the vehicle of characteristics belonging to the listeners, Mind Only, and the Middle Way.

3. The Practice of Meditative Absorption

Not only are the calm abiding meditations that are based on the unique methods of mantra deeply meaningful and easy to practice, the way they are practiced is also common to the sūtra approach. In both cases, one must gain the stability of a pliant mind and then proceed to develop it in a progressive manner.

Moreover, by relying on the eight formative mental states that dispel the five flaws, one uses the six powers to meditate step-by-step on the nine methods for resting the mind. This takes place within the context of the four types of attention, allowing one to gradually produce the five experiences of meditative concentration and, thereby, accomplish the pliancy of calm abiding.

The Five Flaws

The five flaws that inhibit meditative concentration are (1) laziness, (2) forgetting the instructions, (3) dullness and agitation, (4) failure to apply their antidotes, and (5) applying these antidotes even though one is not dull or agitated. Of these, the first two prevent the initial stages of entering absorption, the third hinders the main practice of absorption, and the last two prevent absorption from deepening.

The Eight Remedies

There are eight remedies that dispel these flaws: (1) faith, (2) yearning, (3) exertion, (4) proficiency, (5) mindfulness, (6) introspection, (7) attention, and (8) equanimity. The first four dispel laziness. Faith in the attainment of absorption produces yearning and sincere interest. This, in turn, spurs one to exert oneself, and one thereby becomes proficient and abandons laziness. Mindfulness ensures that the instructions are not forgotten, while introspection allows one to notice when dullness and agitation occur. When they do, attention enables one to apply their respective antidotes. As dullness and agitation subside, one rests in equanimity without forming any concepts. In this way, these eight factors remedy forgetting the instructions and the rest of the faults in a progressive manner.

The Six Powers
Six powers are required to practice absorption in this manner: (1) study, (2) contemplation, (3) mindfulness, (4) introspection, (5) diligence, and (6) complete familiarity. These powers should gradually accomplish the nine methods for resting the mind within the context of the four types of attention.

The Four Types of Attention
The four types of attention are: (1) concentrated attention, (2) occasional attention, (3) uninterrupted attention, and (4) effortless attention.

The Nine Methods for Resting the Mind
The nine methods for resting the mind are: (1) settling, (2) continuous settling, (3) resettling, (4) completely settling, (5) taming, (6) pacifying, (7) completely pacifying, (8) attentiveness, and (9) equipoise. These nine are mentioned in a sūtra, which states, "settling, genuinely settling, collecting and settling, thoroughly settling, taming, pacifying, thoroughly pacifying, one-pointed, and absorbed." To elaborate, study leads to settling; contemplation to continuous settling; mindfulness to resettling and completely settling; introspection to taming and pacifying; diligence to completely pacifying and one-pointedness; and complete familiarity leads to equipoise. In this regard, the first attention relates to the occasion of the first two mental states; the second attention to the third to seventh; the third attention to the eighth; and the fourth to the ninth.

These nine states are also said to unfold by way of five experiences. First is the experience of *movement*, which is like a cascading waterfall. Second is the experience of *attainment*, which is like a river gushing through a gorge. Third is the experience of *familiarity*, which is like the flow of a large river. Fourth is the experience of *stability*, which is like a wave-free ocean. Fifth is the experience of *completion*, which is like a mountain.

Next I will offer practical key instructions that accord with the essential points of these principles.

1. Settling

First, instructions are given on the shortcomings of not attaining meditative concentration, the benefits of attaining it, and the way to rest the mind. Hearing this arouses faith, yearning, and a very disciplined effort, whereby one is rid of laziness and other such faults. Attention is then placed on the observed object according to the systems of development and completion. This is the first method of *settling*.

2. Continuous Settling

When this takes place, one's attention will not rest for even a moment. Instead, it will move around like lightning. Still, one should give rise to a joyful persistence and continue the training. All possible effort should be put into continuously settling on the initial observed object, contemplating the meaning of the instructions on absorption that one has received. This is the second method of *continuous settling*.

3. Resettling

It may be difficult to rest continuously when practicing these first two methods. However, with concentration and focused attention, one will be able to develop continuity. Whenever the mind moves about like a shooting star and becomes distracted from its initial observation, one should use mindfulness to gain composure and resettle, as if channeling a strong river. This is the third method of *resettling*.

The experience of *movement* unfolds when practicing these first three methods for resting the mind. This experience may be likened to a piece of paper carried off by a storm, or to a cascading waterfall. Accordingly, since at this point one's thoughts are very strong, it will be hard to find any moments of rest and it may feel as if one is trying to construct a dam in the middle of a fierce river. Nonetheless, one should continue to apply extraordinary effort without losing heart. The wild horse of the mind is exceedingly difficult to tame; it must be tightly bound with the rope of mindfulness, placed in the corral of carefree equanimity, and steered with the bridle of diligence.

4. Completely Settling

Once one's mindfulness increases slightly in strength, one will be able to rest one's attention on the observed object, although merely in a vague manner. This is the beginning of lesser mental stability. At this time, one's attention should be directed one-pointedly inward so one can settle fully on the observed object alone. This is the fourth method of *completely settling*.

This occasion is similar to birds circling around a carcass. As they hover in the air, they do not move away from the carcass once they have their eyes on it. However, once they descend on the meal, they are unable to remain there and continue to fly around and circle the carcass. In the same way, at this stage one's mind begins to slightly circle its observed object. Hence, the most important thing at this point is to strengthen the continuity of mindfulness.

5. Taming

As one naturally develops a small measure of joy in meditative absorption, one's interest in resting the mind will grow. This is likened to a bee that quickly flies around and drinks nectar without staying in one place for long. At this stage, one will be able to tame slightly the endless conceptual movements prevalent in prior stages. This is the fifth method of *taming*.

Compared to the initial stages, it is somewhat easier to rest one's mind during the stages of completely settling and taming. For this reason, they are also referred to as "the experience of attainment." This is also the very beginning of the initial development of meditative absorption, or the attainment of slight warmth. Exemplified by a river flowing through a gorge, this state involves many subtle concepts that form a continuous, strong turbulence. Nevertheless, as the examples show, compared to the waterfall, the river in the gorge is slightly calmer.

When a bee is caught in a bottle, it has nowhere else to go until freed. Nevertheless, it will continue to move about inside the bottle without settling down. In the same way, in the context of taming when the mind is directed toward an observed object, the mind will not lose its observed object, yet the constant movement of conceptual activity will remain. At this point, it is important to be attentive and not waver from this state of observation.

6. Pacifying

To eliminate dullness and agitation, one should remain mindful while resting attentively. This will allow one to apply their respective remedies in the correct manner so that the variety of concepts that hinder this process may be naturally reduced and pacified. This is the sixth method of *pacifying*.

7. Completely Pacifying

Once this process elicits a peaceful state, it will be as though the muddy water of dullness and agitation has been purified and these faults have disappeared. Like someone recovered from an illness, one will rest attentively and undisturbed in a state of equanimity. The previous slight pacification of thoughts will be strengthened and thoughts will now be clearly distinguished. Even the secondary disturbing emotions will be nearly pacified, like muddy water gradually purified. Distraction, moreover, will no longer occur. This is the seventh method of *completely pacifying*.

The experience of meditation that occurs once the fault of distraction is left behind during the two stages of pacifying and completely pacifying is said to be like a river. From afar, a gently flowing river may appear to be unmoving, but from its bank it will be seen to be in constant motion. In the same way, even though the mind may appear to be settled, careful observation will reveal the occurrence of many subtle fluctuations. At this point, it is crucial to be diligent and develop this further.

8. Attentive

From the stage of *resettling* all the way up to this point, it is necessary to be attentive by engaging the observed object every time dullness and agitation create obstacles. Consequently, the major key point is to tame oneself as much as possible through introspection, contemplation, and equanimity. By mustering diligence, one will now be more advanced than before. So long as one does not forsake exertion, thoughts will be unable to create obstacles and one will rest one-pointedly on the observed object. This stage, referred to as being *attentive* or *one-pointed*, is the eighth method. The experience that comes through gaining stability in this is said to be like a wave-free ocean.

9. Resting in Equanimity

At this stage, one will be able to rest on the observed object and attention will be maintained uninterruptedly through exertion. It is important to rest in equanimity on the observed object at this point. As attention continues to develop, one will no longer need to expend any effort. Instead, a self-perpetuating state of equanimity will occur. This ninth and final method is the attainment of mental rest. This state, also known as "the one-pointed mind of the desire realm," is attained through the process of familiarization and experience that occurs on the preceding levels.

The final mountain-like experience of immutability begins to unfold at this point. When this one-pointed mind of the desire realm is accomplished, the mind blends effortlessly with the observed object that has been held in mind. Throughout all activities, the mind will now rest automatically. If the mind is allowed to rest on its own without thinking, appearances will cease and an experience will occur in which it seems as though one's mind and space have blended. When emerging from this experience, it will feel as though the body has suddenly materialized, and attachment, anger, and other emotions will weaken and become less frequent during the ensuing attainment.

At this point, various experiences of bliss, clarity, and nonthought may occur. During intense experiences of clarity, for example, it may feel as if one can even count the subtle particles within pillars and other such objects. It may also seem as though one's sleep has mingled with meditative absorption, while dreams, for the most part, will be purified. Since this type of meditative absorption can relate to the features of either the truths or subtlety and crudeness, it forms the basis for the common path of both non-Buddhists and Buddhists. As such, it is something one should accomplish. Nevertheless, unless it is imbued with pliancy, it will not be true calm abiding, much less insight. Moreover, one should be aware that the meditative experiences of bliss, clarity, and nonthought may or may not involve equipoise in suchness. One should, therefore, know the key points of the path and not conceitedly take a few experiences of the resting mind to be a sublime path.

By familiarizing oneself with this state of the one-pointed mind of the desire realm, the body and mind will become pliable, an achievement referred to as "proficiency." Once the mind has been tamed like a horse, one will become one's own master and be able to engage a virtuous focus for as long as one wishes. In being free from assuming negative states, such as the unpleasantness of weariness, one will be happy. This, in turn, will cause positive energy to spread throughout the body, ridding it of the negativity that impairs its functioning, such as feelings of physical heaviness. The spine will be straight like a stack of golden coins and the body will feel as light as cotton. One will also feel blissful, as though a stream of warm milk is suddenly filling the entire body. The body, moreover, will become exceedingly pliable and capable of engaging in any virtuous activity.

In the beginning, this type of advanced pliability will occur at a gross level, and then grow increasingly subtle. This gross pliability will start out small before eventually manifesting clearly and completely. Since gross pliability causes the mind to stir, the mind gradually diminishes in strength. Then a subtle and delicate shadow-like pliability will appear that accords with unmoving meditative absorption. This is what we refer to as "calm abiding." Whether one trains in the development or completion stage, this approach will ensure that one's practice is genuine. The teaching on this system constitutes the elaborate explanation of the practice of meditative absorption.

Absorption can also be summarized as follows: With enthusiasm directed toward meditative absorption, attention should be placed on the observed object. One then exerts oneself uninterruptedly, maintaining mindfulness continuously and dispelling dullness and agitation through introspection. When free of faults, one will remain in equanimity. Practicing repeatedly with enthusiasm, exertion, mindfulness, introspection, and equanimity will lead you naturally to a state of nondistraction. The practice will finally be accomplished once you can rest well without any movement. Alternatively, you can practice in a fourfold manner by settling with enthusiasm, giving rise to effort, guarding with introspection, and resting in equanimity; or in an even more condensed manner by simply settling on the observed object as long as you can. Thus, there are several levels of instructions.

4. Purpose

The meaning ascertained by the view of great purity and equality can only be applied correctly to one's own being once the strength of meditative absorption has been perfected. For this reason, meditative absorption is extremely important. It is the primary cause for accomplishing activity and spiritual attainments, both of which require awareness and stability. Still, even though there are many who conceitedly profess to have attained the noble path through platitudes and empty words, it is rare to find someone who has accomplished even the one-pointed mind of the desire realm. The current scarcity of people practicing even the smallest activity of mantra is due to a lack of meditative absorption. Therefore, those who wish for activities and spiritual attainments should persevere in meditative absorption.

In short, through meditative absorption one can engage the meaning of the view. As one progresses, conduct manifests. This is also how one observes the samayas and what makes the maṇḍala appear. If one possesses meditative absorption, one can grant empowerment, gain accomplishment, perform activities, and make offerings. Meditative absorption is what blesses mantra and mudrā. Thus, it encompasses all of these factors. As one gains confidence in the meaning that all phenomena are great purity and equality by their very nature, one will move beyond the boundaries of meditation and nonmeditation. This effortless and spontaneously present practice is the consummation of the great perfection.

The *Tantra of the Secret Essence* says:

> The way of utterly pure basic space is itself
> Mastery of this and enjoyment of that.
> Therefore, self, other, and the continuity of concepts
> Are purified in the supreme, unsurpassed vehicle.

The *Gathering of Secrets* says:

> As there are no entities, there is no meditation.
> Meditation is nonmeditation itself.
> As such, these entities and nonentities
> Are not observed in meditation.

This concludes the explanation of meditative absorption, the perfection of meditative concentration.

3. Conduct
Conduct is discussed in terms of its (1) essence, (2) divisions, (3) principles, and (4) purpose.

1. Essence

> The spiritual attainments of the mantra-wielding practitioner
> Are spontaneously present as perfect equality.

Since conduct is utterly unimpeded,
Everything is primordially indivisible.

Conduct is a translation of the Sanskrit word *carya*. This term refers to all physical, verbal, and mental actions of a mantra practitioner who correctly engages in the tasks to be performed while embracing his or her conduct with unique methods and knowledge.

2. Divisions

In terms of support, conduct can be divided into physical, verbal, and mental acts. In terms of its essence, there is a twofold division: the disciplined conduct of the path of means and the conscientious conduct of the path of liberation. The former refers to the general common activities and the special activities of union and liberation. Concerning the latter, on the path of liberation there are seven types of conduct, including the conduct of having faith and being diligent. These forms of conduct are for individuals of a gradual inclination. There is also said to be an eighth activity, conduct free from acceptance and rejection, which is meant for individuals of an instantaneous inclination. There are also a great number of other ways to divide conduct. One such example is the training in absorption during meditative equipoise and seeing all appearances as illusion during the ensuing attainment, whereby one freely enjoys the sense pleasures. Nevertheless, conduct is normally classified under the rubric of the ensuing attainment.

There are also various activities that relate to the process of attaining internal heat and progressing in practice. One set of divisions classifies conduct using the terms elaborate, unelaborate, and extremely unelaborate. Another classification is made in terms of the youthful activity of beginning mendicants, the disciplined conduct of a madman able to bear hardships, and the royal activity of a ruler who has attained stability. Yet another system speaks of the conduct of vibration and the ever-excellent conduct of universal victory. In this way, there are numerous systems for naming and classifying conduct.

In terms of time, there are three forms of conduct: the initial conduct of engagement, the interim conduct of attaining the spiritual attainments, and the final conduct of accomplishment. The first of these refers to serving the master, receiving empowerment, upholding the samayas, receiving instructions on practice, and not transgressing the guru's command. The second division refers to the various aspects of approach and accomplishment. The third, the conduct of accomplishment, refers to all the applications of activity subsequent to the achievement of the spiritual attainments. These three divisions encompass all the paths of the vajra vehicle.

3. Principles

This section has a general and a specific discussion. Concerning the first, one may think, "In the common vehicles, the sense pleasures are taught to be obstacles to the path. Why is it that here they are to be taken up?" Since all phenomena dwell as the great bliss of equality and purity, there is nothing to observe in terms of accepting or rejecting. The path of abiding in whatever one desires in harmony with the realization of this nature bestows liberation quickly and easily, like magic. Moreover, with this approach liberation does not require acts of asceticism or other forms of hardship. Such acts only create obstacles. For this reason, it is said to be a root downfall if a mantra practitioner feels contempt for and mortifies his or her own body. Therefore, although one joyfully partakes in sense pleasures, this approach is superior to the common vehicles because one applies the key points of masterful methods and nondeluded knowledge. *The Vajra Ḍākinī* states:

> The horrible ties of ascetic discipline
> Deprive the body and create misery.
> Misery will only distract the mind,
> And distraction transforms the spiritual attainments.

The *Yoginī Tantra of Conduct* explains:

> When in possession of the nondual wisdom mind,
> There is nothing forbidden at all.
> With a nonconceptual mind,
> The five sense pleasures are enjoyed.

The End of Magic states:

> The fruition of nonduality
> Is not attained after innumerable eons
> Of painful ascetic discipline,
> But in this life, through happiness and pleasure.

Not only that, even a sūtra says:

> Just as the manure of the city dwellers' excrement
> Benefits fields of sugarcane,
> The manure of a bodhisattva's disturbing emotions
> Benefits the accomplishment of the Buddha's teachings.

The specific discussion establishes the principles of union through knowledge and liberation through method. Concerning the first, some individuals enter the vehicle of mantra but nevertheless fail to take an interest in the magnificent conduct of mantra and scorn the practice of union. This is a grave mistake. As a cause for the sudden dawning of co-emergent wisdom, the karma mudrā and the supportive jasmine-like bodhicitta are indispensable. To give them up is, therefore, said to be a root downfall of mantra. Union, moreover, is said to be the wonderful conduct of knowledge.

The meaning of the co-emergent, natural state, which the common paths take innumerable eons to realize, dwells primordially within oneself. It is directly perceived through these methods by intelligent people who are knowledgeable about the essential points of the teacher's key instructions. With this knowledge, all dualistic thoughts are bound within the nondual state of basic space and wisdom, hence the term "nondual union." On this topic, the *Great Bliss Union of the Buddhas* states:

> Among all wonders,
> The wonder of the female is the greatest.

And in the *Saṃbhuṭa*:

> Therefore, what is the use of anything more extensive?
> For the concise leads to buddhahood itself.
> The very buddhahood that is attained
> Through countless billions of eons,
> Through this sacred bliss
> Can be attained in this very life.

Likewise, the *Tantra of the Single Ferocious Hero* states:

> There is no evil greater than action without desire.
> There is no merit greater than bliss.
> Therefore, settle the mind in equipoise
> And give rise to the bliss of desire.

Again, the *Compendium of Vajra Wisdom* explains:

> Without the manifest conditioning of milk and sesame seeds, butter and sesame oil do not form. Likewise, without joining the vajra and the lotus, which are manifestly conditioned by mantra and mudrā, the three cognitions cannot be illustrated. One will not achieve the absorption of great bliss without being able to genuinely join the bhaga and liṅga. Simply by having intense interest exclusively in the absorption of great bliss will lead one to the level of a beginner and the training of a nonreturner.

Second, neither should one have misgivings about the supreme method of liberation. There are individuals who turn away from the three jewels, accumulate the gravest of negative actions, and for whom no other remedy works. Consequently, that person will forever wander without refuge in the lower realms. However, if one is motivated by an unparalleled compassion, one can sever the continuity of the life force of these individuals with negative karma using the profound method of mantra and liberate them with ease.

In this way, a practitioner with confidence in the view of equality who has perfected the strength of training in the two stages is able to capture the life force of the liberated one and bring about the fruition of the triple satisfaction. Such potent conduct can be of great benefit to both oneself and others and is more marvelous and amazing than other forms of conduct in the mantra tradition. It is said that if one fails to perform this sort of liberation when the time is right, one will be committing a root downfall. Moreover, having understood this correctly, even a mere interest in this practice will bring innumerable benefits.

These days there are many people who ferociously brandish their kīla dagger at a dough effigy, but few are those who can summon the cause—severe karma and disturbing emotions—and the result—the beings of the three lower realms—into the support and then apply themselves in a genuine manner to transference by means of the mantric ritual of liberation. Nevertheless, even if one merely performs an approximation of the liberation ritual innumerable benefits will still occur. Since one relies on a motivation of unparalleled compassion and a conduct that is skilled in the methods of mantra, this is unequaled by common forms of mind training and ordinary meditation practices.

The *Compendium of Secrets* explains further:

> Those who despise the vajra master,
> And those who revile the great and supreme vehicle
> Should be killed with great effort
> Or removed from this place.
> In this way, one attains supreme enlightenment,
> The accomplishment of mantra.

While the *Tantra of Red Yamantaka* states:

> Oh! Those to be killed are benefited,
> For the victim is not killed.
> So long as they are caused to be liberated from sin,
> The one who passes away will not die.
>
> Those who have committed a thousand sins
> Will not be born in hells such as Ultimate Torment.
> Amazing! A great being attains buddhahood
> And enlightenment through killing.
>
> Again, with love, kill sentient beings
> Who should be killed!
> Amazing! It is accomplished through the power
>   of compassion,
> Not through inferior compassion.

The *Root Section of the Kīla Tantra* says:

> The samaya of liberating with compassion
> Is not killing and suppressing.

> The aggregates are filled with vajras,
> And consciousness is meditated on as a vajra.

In this way, one should stop disrespecting the deep practices of mantra and instead give rise to an attitude of the utmost respect, with a realization of their profound key points.

4. Purpose

In general, the purpose of conduct is to attain the temporal and ultimate spiritual attainments. Specifically, in relevant situations, profound conduct with a proximate cause supremely enhances realization within one's being, through which one quickly attains buddhahood. In short, conduct refers to all the various activities of the ensuing attainment that are in harmony with the practice of view and meditation. It also includes entering and meditating on the profound maṇḍala, drawing images of the maṇḍala, receiving and bestowing empowerment, abiding by the samayas, performing approach and accomplishment, making offerings to please the deities, accomplishing enlightened activity, reciting mantras, and holding mudrās. Since these are all instances of conduct, conduct encompasses them all.

Ultimately, all appearances and activities—whatever appears and is done—are exclusively the play of reality, the indivisible truths of purity and equality. When this is experienced, one transcends the extremes of action and nonaction. To naturally sustain this innate conduct of self-manifestation and self-liberation is the conduct of practitioners of the great perfection. This is the culmination of all forms of conduct. On this topic, the *Tantra of the Secret Essence* states:

> Primordially unborn suchness
> Is illusory in appearance like an apparition.
> Though union, liberation, and all other acts
> Are performed, not the slightest thing is done.

Through this, one will be patient when it comes to undertaking the profound activities of mantra. As this form of patience engages in all appearances and activities as the play of wisdom, it is said to be the perfection of patience.

This concludes the explanation of conduct.

4. Maṇḍala

Maṇḍala will be discussed in terms of its (1) essence, (2) divisions, (3) principle, and (4) purpose.

1. Essence

> From nonseparation comes separation.
> The inner and external-inner maṇḍalas
> Are the inconceivable play of wisdom,
> The supreme mudrā of the fearless Samantabhadra.

In Sanskrit, *maṇḍa* means "essence" or "quintessence," while *la* means to "hold" or "uphold." Thus, the word means "the ground that holds essential qualities." Alternatively, if one takes the word as a whole and directly translates it, it means "completely round" or "full circle." For this reason, it is called *kyilkhor* ("center and circle") in Tibetan, referring to a chief figure surrounded by a retinue, or the Transcendent Conqueror Dharma King, along with his retinue and palace. Hence, in this context, a maṇḍala is the ground that upholds supreme qualities and appears as the embodiment of the completely pure support and supported.

2. Divisions

Maṇḍalas can be divided in terms of ground, path, and fruition. The natural maṇḍala of the ground refers to the primordial divine nature of the world and its inhabitants, the support and supported. This can be divided further, starting with the maṇḍala of a single family and all the way up to the maṇḍala of the inconceivable magical net. Its essence, the indivisible truths of purity and equality, arises as the unimpeded array that assists those in need.

The maṇḍala of meditation on the path consists of the symbolic representational maṇḍala and the symbolized actual maṇḍala of enlightened body, speech, and mind. The former refers to maṇḍalas of colored sand, paintings, drawings, and heaps. As for the latter, the maṇḍala of enlightened body is one's own body visualized as a deity—from a sole hero to the entire maṇḍala with deities and a palace. The maṇḍala of enlightened speech is the visualization of the mantras of the central deity and the retinue, and the recitation of the mantra. The maṇḍala of enlightened mind is to bring the five poisons onto the path as the five wisdoms, thus not abandoning saṃsāra, but bringing about a fundamental purification.

The maṇḍala of the perfected fruition is the state in which the bodies are without meeting and parting once the path has been perfected and the state of Samantabhadra has been attained.

Further divisions can also be made, such as the maṇḍalas of the three bodies, the maṇḍalas of the five wisdoms, and the maṇḍalas of enlightened body, speech, mind, qualities, and activities. There are other classifications as well, including a sevenfold division, but these are all subsumed under the aforementioned maṇḍalas of enlightened body, speech, and mind.

Another threefold classification is as follows: The maṇḍala of the support is the palace. This maṇḍala is arrayed in various directions and completely surrounds a center—the perfect place. The maṇḍala of the supported refers to deities and consists of a main deity surrounded by his or her divine retinue—the perfect teacher and retinue. The nondual great wisdom maṇḍala consists of self-occurring wisdom and a retinue of mindful cognition. Moreover, the indwelling wisdom, free from any instigating dualistic conceptual fluctuations, is taught to be Samantabhadra. The concepts that emerge from this state, such as the five poisons, are taught to be the expression of wisdom in the form of the forty-two buddhas, such as the five thus-gone ones. The stillness and fluctuations of awareness are said to be the primordial maṇḍala. This constitutes the perfect teaching and time. There are also numerous other ways to make divisions, such as the three maṇḍalas of nature, meditative absorption, and symbols, and the four vajra maṇḍalas of enlightened body, speech, mind, and wisdom.

The latter section of the *Tantra of the Secret Essence* presents seven maṇḍalas:

> This teaches the natural maṇḍala,
> Representations, exalted representations,
> Meditative absorption, superior meditative absorption,
> Awakened mind, and supreme assembly.

The natural maṇḍala can be divided into the maṇḍala of the ground, which is the natural state of primordial purity of all phenomena, and the maṇḍala of the consummate fruition, which refers to the actualized ground, as it is, once one is free of temporary stains. In reality, however, the maṇḍala of great purity and equality, in which ground and fruition are indivisible, is the unfabricated and spontaneously present natural maṇḍala.

Second is the representative maṇḍala. This refers to the appearances of the impure phenomena of saṃsāra, which are so-called because their essence is primordially pure and their features resemble the pure support and supported.

Third is the superior representative maṇḍala. This is the form of the palace made from colored sand, and other things that illustrate the pure support and supported. These symbolic signs—such as statues, scriptures, and stūpas—are more exalted than the signs of saṃsāra in a conventional sense, which is why they are called the superior representative maṇḍala.

There are three stages to drawing a superior representative maṇḍala for use in an empowerment ritual or sādhana practice: the preliminaries, main part, and conclusion. For the preliminaries, one should first analyze the area by investigating the sky, ground, and atmosphere. If the place is deemed suitable, one should then request permission to use it from the owner, whether apparent or not. Next, one should imagine the ritual dagger to be the Lotus Kīlaya and use it as a stake to subdue the area. Then one should look for snakes, hide treasures, and make the area level. The place should then be purified through plastering, fire offering, mantra, mudrā, and absorption. Next, the boundaries should be set with the five types of weapons, thereby protecting the land. As the light that shines from the play of the male and female deities dissolves into the ground, one should imagine that it becomes the nature of the maṇḍala and, in this way, takes hold of the ground. These six successive activities transform the ground into a suitable place to draw a maṇḍala.

For the main part of the practice, assemble the kīla for blessing, along with threads and colored powder. Next, correctly perform the progressive tasks, such as circling the area with a qualified companion. In this way, establish the size of the maṇḍala with demarcation threads, apply the colors, arrange the symbols, perform the consecration, make various offerings to the maṇḍala, and conclude with a fire offering. These five acts will make it a suitable basis for accomplishment. The conclusion consists of all the stages of activity, such as entering the maṇḍala and conferring empowerment upon disciples.

Fourth is the maṇḍala of meditative absorption. Here one takes the natural maṇḍala as one's object of meditation, referring to the indivisibility of all phenomena, which are the embodiment of enlightened body, speech, and mind.

Fifth is the maṇḍala of superior meditative absorption. This involves meditating by attaining clear appearance in the thoroughly complete and distinct forms of the support and supported elements of any given maṇḍala, whether peaceful and compassionate or wrathful and demon taming. These are the specific qualities that appear from the ground. Here one progresses through the preliminaries, main part, and conclusion as outlined in the practice manual one is using.

Sixth is the maṇḍala of the awakened mind. This refers to the actual dawn of the co-emergent wisdom of great bliss that dwells within, which occurs by bringing the channels, energies, and essences onto the path. This is the most sacred of the maṇḍalas of the path.

Seventh is the maṇḍala of the group gathering. This refers to a gathering of male and female practitioners of deity meditation for the purpose of profound accomplishment.

3. Principle

What we refer to as a "maṇḍala" embodies the entire meaning of ground, path, and fruition of the vajra vehicle. For this reason, it should be known, practiced, and attained; the natural maṇḍala of the ground should be known, the meditation maṇḍala of the path should be practiced in training, and the wisdom maṇḍala of the fruition should be attained.

The maṇḍala is also the essence of what should be known, the essence of what should be practiced, and the essence of what should be attained. Since no phenomenon within appearance and existence lies beyond the meaning of the indivisible truths of the ground continuum, the maṇḍala is the essence of that which is to be known. The maṇḍala to be practiced is also the essence, or entity, of all the trainings found on the path. Since ground and fruition are inseparable, all the appearances that pertain to the ground and path are in actuality spontaneously present as the essence of the fruition, that which is to be attained.

Alternatively, it can also be said that the maṇḍala is not something to be known, not something to be practiced, and not something to be attained. The ground, the natural state of the indivisible truths of purity and equality, is beyond words, thought, and description. It is, therefore, also beyond conceptual mind. In this way, it is not something that can be known as an observed object. As it is primordially present, there is no need to practice it now through the path. Moreover, since even those phenomena that are to be practiced are nonexistent when examined, it is not something to practice. Since it is spontaneously present and has been from the beginning, it is not something that can be attained anew, nor is it something to attain, since ultimately no phenomena to be attained can be held in mind.

In this way, the mind that sees the profound meaning of the two truths—that in terms of the way things conventionally appear there is something to accomplish, while in terms of their true, ultimate nature there is not—is said to "unerringly accomplish everything." This is how one should understand the maṇḍala.

4. Purpose

For great beings to accomplish the dharma kingdom, the primary cause is the dharma king. Therefore, the maṇḍala is extremely important; all paths of mantra appear based on this, and all paths and fruitions become its essence. In short, this maṇḍala should be known through the view and established as the basis for meditation practice. Even the conduct should not depart from it. It is the site for the appearance of empowerment, the basis for what should be performed in practice, the recipient of offerings, the foundation for enlightened activity, mantra, and mudrā, and that which the samayas should observe. In this way, it encompasses all areas of training. Since the state of the spontaneously present natural maṇḍala is perfected without any action or effort, it is consummate. The *Tantra of the Secret Essence* explains:

> Wisdom is represented through four directions and a center;
> This inconceivable and spontaneously present maṇḍala is the great perfection.
> The practitioner who realizes this
> Enjoys everything as the natural and great maṇḍala.

Since this shows how wisdom's self-displays manifest as the form of the maṇḍala, the topic of the maṇḍala is explained to be the perfection of wisdom.

5. Empowerment

Empowerment is presented in terms of its (1) essence, (2) divisions, (3) principle, and (4) purpose.

1. Essence

> When the disciplined conduct of faith and diligence is fully realized,
> The beneficial empowerments and the potent empowerments
> Should be conferred in a gradual manner.
> Through compassion, uphold without wasting.

The Sanskrit word for empowerment is *abhiṣiñca*. Etymologically, *abhi* means "manifest" and *ṣiñca* means "to scatter" or "to pour." Accordingly, the meaning is that the profound ritual of conferring empowerment washes, or scatters, the stains of the disciple's body, speech, mind, and their combination, and establishes, or pours, an extraordinary capacity into the disciple's being, whereby he or she may develop the wisdom that ripens this into the four vajras.

2. Divisions

There are four empowerments that serve to remove the stains of the four occasions at the time of the ground, allow one to train in the four paths, and attain the four bodies at the time of the fruition. The vase empowerment purifies the body and channels into the emanation body. The secret empowerment purifies the speech and energies into the enjoyment body. The wisdom-knowledge empowerment purifies the mind and the essences into the dharma body. The word empowerment purifies the combination of body, speech, and mind into the essence body. The latter section of the *Tantra of the Secret Essence* says:

> The master, the secret, knowledge,
> And the immediately following, the fourth.

The tantras teach many different configurations for categorizing the four empowerments and their respective, specific rituals. This tantra teaches three empowerments: the beneficial empowerments, the potent empowerments, and the profound empowerments. The profound empowerments can also be contained under the potent empowerments, in which case there are only two classifications. Alternatively, if one divides the profound empowerments into three there are five in total. It is taught that the first of these five plants the seed, the second ripens the capacity, the third produces experience, the fourth brings stability, and the fifth perfects this stability and allows one to achieve the supreme spiritual attainments.

From this perspective, the vase empowerment is divided into both the beneficial empowerments and potent empowerments. There are ten peaceful beneficial empowerments consisting of the five essences, the diadem, and so forth. The wrathful empowerments are known to have twenty-eight divisions, such as those of the seats, the empowerment of the deities, the symbolic implements, and so on. Although these bring benefit, the bestowal of these empowerments does not enable one to immediately engage in the activities of explaining, listening, and practicing mantra, which is why they are called the beneficial empowerments.

There are five potent empowerments. The empowerment of hearing the secret and the empowerment that brings spiritual attainment relate primarily to one's own ability, while the empowerment of explaining the secret and the empowerment ritual of performing enlightened activity relate mainly to the ability of others. The empowerment of the entire teaching of the vajra king is given in relation to the ability of both oneself and others. Although these empowerments are also beneficial, they are called potent empowerments because they emphasize conferring, in a direct manner, the ability to engage in certain activities.

There are three profound empowerments. The secret empowerment is granted to engage in disciplined action, such as partaking in the five meats and five nectars without any sense of their being pure or impure. The wisdom-knowledge empowerment is bestowed upon those engaged in the disciplined action of the consort. The fourth empowerment is bestowed upon those who practice the disciplined action of the equality of all phenomena. These three profound empowerments are also known as the three higher empowerments.

3. Principle

Empowerment is the indispensable initial entry point for the practice of mantra. The reason for this is that the profound empowerment ritual produces a sudden manifestation of the ground maṇḍala that dwells primordially within oneself. This refers to the indivisible truths of purity and equality, which are very difficult to realize. In this way, empowerment is a unique method for maturing the wisdom of the four vajras.

How does empowerment bring about such maturation? From the inconceivable force of the coming together of certain causes and conditions (there are two causes and four conditions), the special realization of profound mantra is either produced in actuality, or the ability to produce it is established in one's being. The resembling cause for this maturation is the great bliss of purity and equality, the reality that indivisibly pervades the disciple's channels, energies, essences, and mind. The concurrent causes are certain substances, such as the vase in the first empowerment, the bodhicitta substance of the master and consort in the second empowerment, the substance of the wisdom consort in the third empowerment, and the substance of symbols and expressions in the fourth empowerment. These are consecrated and blessed through the exceptional realization of the mantric view.

As for the four conditions, the causal condition is a devoted and knowledgeable student who is a suitable recipient for the bestowal of empowerment. The ruling condition is a genuine master who is competent when it comes to the path of mantra and is, therefore, capable of conferring an empowerment that blesses the mind of the disciple. The observed condition consists of substances, mantras, and absorptions of an extraordinary potency. The immediate condition consists of the preceding empowerments and rituals, since the former empowerments open the gate to those that follow.

The power that results from the coming together of these two causes and four conditions causes one's indwelling wisdom to dawn in actuality. This occurs due to the inconceivable force of the unfailing dependent origination of reality itself, which is great bliss, and phenomena; the inconceivable force of the thus-gone ones' blessings; and the inconceivable potency of mantra and mudrā, the unique activities of secret mantra's skillful methods. This is as indisputable as the potency of gems and medicines. The *Kīla Tantra* says:

> The truth of reality,
> The blessings of secret mantra,
> The power of the Buddha ...

Therefore, empowerments enable one to gradually generate understanding, experience, and realization of the meaning of the four vajras. Then, if one genuinely applies oneself to the path that further develops these factors, one will be able to attain the state of vajradhara in just a single life, short as they are in this degenerate age. Even if one does not deliberately strive on the path in this lifetime, it is said that it will not be long before one can become enlightened, so long as one's samayas remain intact.

4. Purpose

The path of mantra, which allows one to attain the state of enlightenment easily and swiftly, comes about from the ripening effect of the empowerment and never from anywhere else. On the path of sūtra, wisdom results from gathering the twofold accumulations on a vast scale for innumerable eons. Through the force of empowerment, in contrast, that wisdom can suddenly enter an ordinary being on the ground of a complete beginner. On this point, it is said:

> It is co-emergent and not expressed by others,
> Nor can it be discovered anywhere.
> It is known through the master's timely and skillful teaching
> And from one's own merit.

Without empowerment, it is improper even to read or listen to the texts of the profound secret tantra, let alone practice them. The *Tantra of the Secret Essence* states:

> To begin study and the like
> Without pleasing the master
> Or receiving empowerment
> Will be fruitless and one will be ruined.

While the *Essence of the Great Seal* explains:

> Without empowerment there will be no spiritual attainments,
> Just as no butter will come from squeezing sand.
> When someone who is arrogant about tantras and scriptures
> Teaches those without empowerment,
> Both master and student will go to hell upon death,
> Even if they have gained spiritual attainment.

On the other hand, if one receives empowerment, the situation is just the opposite. By attaining permission, one can properly engage in all the paths and spiritual attainments of secret mantra. To receive the genuine empowerment of mantra from a master who possesses the blessings of the lineage is, therefore, an indispensable element that will bring about limitless qualities. The *Tantra of the Secret Essence* says:

> Child of the Victorious One, from this day forward,
> All lower realms cease to exist,
> Your life will be long, happy and perfect,
> And you will be a master of the higher realms and liberation.

Moreover, as the tantras mention, simply seeing the maṇḍala has innumerable benefits.

In short, "empowerment" is the sole, initial gateway to all the paths of the vajra vehicle. It is the exceptional method for empowering one into the meditation of the path and the attainment of the fruition. Based on empowerment, the view of mantra is produced in one's being; one can meditate in accordance with that view; be effective in conduct; ensure that the practice, the offerings, the activity, mantra, and mudrā become meaningful; and that the samayas are attained. Therefore, empowerment is like the source of everything. It is like a king in bringing forth the attainment of the progressive states of realization. Thus, everything depends on empowerment.

Ultimately, when one sees that there is nothing to confer or obtain and one is perfectly complete as the great dharma body, one attains the empowerment of the expression of self-awareness in the manner of the great perfection. This is the culmination of all empowerments. About this, the *Tantra of the Secret Essence* states:

> Becoming nondual, the great seal.

As they possess the supreme power to imbue one's being with wisdom, they are the perfection of power.

This concludes the teaching on the topic of empowerment.

6. Samayas

Samayas will be presented in terms of their (1) essence, (2) divisions, (3) principles, and (4) purpose.

1. Essence
The *Tantra of the Secret Essence* states:

> Within the supreme and unsurpassable samaya,
> The discipline through the power of taming
> And all the inconceivable vows, however many there may be,
> Are present without exception and entirely pure.

Samaya vow comes from the Sanskrit term *samaya*, which means something that is not to be transgressed. It also refers to the commands of great beings. Samayas are points of training that masterful practitioners do not transgress, but enact in accordance with what is to be engaged in and rejected.

2. Divisions
Samayas contain both general divisions and specific divisions.

1. General Divisions
In brief, the mantra samayas are condensed into three categories: the general samayas, particular samayas, and superior samayas. General samayas are explained to be the vows of individual liberation, the trainings of the awakened mind, and the samayas of outer mantra. Since these are not to be transgressed without any real purpose, they form the foundation for, and are a facet of, the samayas of unsurpassable mantra. For this reason, they are also called the "common general samayas." The particular samayas are said to be the root and branch samayas that are found throughout the unsurpassable mantra itself.

Alternatively, one may also say that the general samayas are termed "general" because all the vows of individual liberation, the awakened mind, and mantra are to be observed in general. According to the mental strength of the practitioner and the superior or inferior situation one may find oneself in, the samayas are upheld by applying the view, conduct, activity and so forth to one's own meditative experience. Since specific individuals uphold these vows, they are also named "specific samayas." The superior samayas are taught to be the unique vows that are taken during periods of great accomplishment, in addition to those that one should always keep, such as "not destroying the lion's abdomen."

2. Specific Divisions

Other tantras teach the fourteen root downfalls and the eight grave subsidiary downfalls. Moreover, the number of levels and categories within the samayas taught in the individual tantras differ from one another. In this context, fifteen samayas are taught, of which five are root samayas and ten are subsidiary samayas. This approach is the ultimate key point of all the samayas belonging to inner secret mantra. Consequently, if one understands this approach and does not transgress these vows, they will not become damaged. It is, therefore, important to comprehend and observe these key points.

The five root samayas are (1) not discarding the unsurpassable, (2) respecting the master, (3) not disrupting the continuity of mantra and mudrā, (4) loving those who have entered the authentic path, and (5) not explaining the secret meaning to unqualified recipients. The ten subsidiary samayas are not to abandon the five poisons and to readily accept the five nectars.

1. The Five Root Samayas

1. Not Discarding the Unsurpassable

Here, "unsurpassable" refers to the ultimate natural state of all phenomena—the inseparability of the truths of purity and equality, the dharma body. It is called "unsurpassable" because there is no fruition and no path that could possibly surpass this level of realization and attainment. It is, therefore, something to feel great trust in and not something to be discarded. In essence, in not discarding this fruition, one will also not discard the three jewels and the relative and ultimate awakened mind. The Buddha correctly actualized the natural state of the intrinsic nature, just as it is, while the saṅgha has realized it to various degrees. If you have conviction in the unsurpassable and do not discard it, it will be impossible for you to abandon those who see it—the noble ones, the knowledge holders, and the buddhas—as well as the dharma that is present in their beings.

The three jewels of ground, path, and fruition are also included by virtue of their intrinsic nature. At the time of the ground, the mind nature of sentient beings is the buddha in essence. The dharma is inseparable from this essence, just like the sun and its rays, while speech abides as the wheel of syllables. Due to their intrinsic nature, sentient beings are a field for the practice of merit and are, therefore, the saṅgha. In this way, the intrinsic nature is established as the three jewels.

In the context of the path, one's own body, speech, and mind are buddha from the very start, insofar as they are the enlightened body, speech, and mind in identity. The development and completion stages of the path are the dharma, and their practical application is the saṅgha. These factors embody the three jewels in the context of the path.

A buddha who has completed the path, the dharma this buddha teaches, and the saṅgha of practitioners are widely known as the three jewels. Upon attaining buddhahood, the Capable One possesses the dharma body and his training has reached a point of completion. Therefore, he embodies the threefold refuge of the fruition.

In this way, all three jewels of the ground, path, and fruition are not different from the single mode of the inseparable truths of purity and equality. This is the three jewels of the ultimate natural state, in which everything is perfected as equality. Therefore, in upholding the unsurpassable, one upholds everything.

There are two ways of upholding the unsurpassable. One may uphold it out of devotion, thinking that it must be as taught in the scriptures, although one may not have gained certainty oneself. Alternatively, one may uphold it out of certainty by gaining conviction in the meaning of the view and understanding that it cannot be discarded since it is the way things primordially are. The latter of these two is irreversible, in the sense that even if one has entered an inferior path, this certainty has the power to cause one to reverse course. Therefore, anyone who possesses such a view is called a "vajra holder" because, by maintaining the vajra-like reality of mantra in one's being, such a person will be able to overcome all forms of degeneration within both cyclic existence and peace.

Furthermore, because one will have apprehended the ultimate, final, natural state, the inseparability of the truths of purity and equality, the ultimate awakened mind will not be lost. Moreover, because one never forsakes the motivation and actions of attaining enlightenment to protect all sentient beings from their miseries, the relative awakened mind will not be lost either. Seeing with certainty that this attainment of enlightenment involves constantly and pervasively working for the welfare of the infinite number of sentient beings, all the defilements that relate to directing one's mind to inferior paths, such as turning the mind away from this approach, faint-heartedness, aversion towards saṃsāra, and so on, are utterly stopped. A tantra states:

> I and all the countless sentient beings
> Have been buddhas from the very start.
> As the embodiment of this recognition,
> I give rise to the supreme awakened mind.

Some individuals hold that the fruition of buddhahood is established only through the power of a causal path. While such people do indeed generate the awakened mind, feelings of discouragement, self-interest, and weariness with saṃsāra, and other such attitudes could cause them to lose their resolve. In this way, it is possible that this could hinder the cause. Buddhahood will not be achieved if all the right causes are not in place, just as a sprout cannot grow from a burnt seed. Consequently, enlightenment is seen to depend solely on one's own power. Moreover, because the mind depends on conditions, ordinary beings do not attain a completely stable confidence, but simply a firm commitment to generating the awakened mind.

In the context of mantra, however, one is clear about how to develop the relative and ultimate awakened mind inseparably. Therefore, even at the level of an ordinary being, one gives rise to a supreme confidence that even the relative awakened mind cannot be abandoned. This shows that even a beginner who has engaged with the reality of mantra is as fortunate as a nonreturning bodhisattva.

The reality of unsurpassable mantra is the ultimate deity of reality itself. All the deities that manifest in symbolic mudrā forms are accomplished by not discarding this ultimate deity. By upholding the life force of all samayas and meditation practices with this view, they will remain pure and never degenerate. Therefore, if one possesses the view, which is a deep-felt certainty in the meaning of the unsurpassable reality of mantra, it is impossible for the essential point of the root samayas to degenerate.

Still, those who have entered mantra out of mere devotion may give up on the unsurpassable. They may lose faith in the meaning of the profound view of the inseparability of purity and equality, as well as the stable trainings of mantra that accord with this view. As taught in the fourteen root downfalls, turning one's back on these is a downfall. Moreover, such an individual may also fall prey to doubts, thinking that the meaning of the divine purity of the environment and inhabitants is merely taught for the purpose of guiding those in need, while in reality they are not pure. They may also think that the meaning of equality possesses referential attributes, thereby clinging to something that is not actually great equality. With these two fundamental downfalls, one has effectively turned one's back on the view of mantra. Therefore, since they are in total conflict with the reality of mantra arising in one's being, they are both root downfalls.

Such individuals may also do things that conflict with the wonderful conduct of mantra, such as mortifying the aggregates, not delighting in the samaya substances, relinquishing the awakened mind that is like a jasmine flower, disparaging women, and not liberating those who should be liberated. These all amount to turning one's back with utter aversion on the practices that should be adopted. This effectively eliminates the good fortune needed to practice the profound conduct of mantra. Hence, these too are root downfalls.

The other downfalls are set forth in relation to the master who directly teaches the profound meaning of mantra; one's relatives who uphold the meaning of mantra; sentient beings who are to be tamed through mantra; keeping secrecy to avoid breaking the continuity of mantra; the words of the Victorious One that either directly or indirectly teach the very meaning of mantra; the teachings of masters; and the various philosophies that allow for analysis of the various parameters of mantra. Through their connection with the perfect view and conduct of mantra, these areas are established to be equally sacred. By not showing them due respect, one is squandering mantra itself. This is why they are posited as root downfalls. Therefore, not properly observing these points, such as respecting the teacher and teaching mantra in secrecy, is a great fault. For this reason, they are listed and taught in the tantras of mantra. If these principles are violated, one will not be in harmony with mantra and, thus, also be in conflict with the conduct of mantra. As these fourteen are in great conflict with the view and conduct of mantra, they alone are taught to be root downfalls.

Therefore, even though one's understanding of the view and conduct of mantra may not be based on direct experience, one should never disparage it, for doing so would be the extremely awful fault of having abandoned the dharma. For those who have received empowerment, this is a root downfall.

There is, however, no problem if one is unable to practice the profound activities of mantra immediately upon receiving empowerment. Still, one should aspire to practice these activities, thinking that in the future one will joyfully take them up by whatever means necessary. Never should one's back be turned on them! Moreover, even though one has not attained certainty in the profound views, one should aspire to them, thinking that they should by all means dawn in one's being because they are the ultimate profound intent of the vajra vehicle. It is inappropriate to think that they are incorrect and discard them. Consider the following lines from the *Lesser Saṃvara Tantra*:

> Even if one does not aspire to
> The teachings of the profound doctrine,
> One should not disparage them,
> But recall that reality is inconceivable.
>
> The one for whom this is not an object
> Is one who does not know of reality.
> It is known by great beings—
> The buddhas and their offspring.

2. Respecting the Master

Generally speaking, all qualities of the path depend on a spiritual friend. The sūtras teach that one should view the spiritual friend as a buddha. In particular, without relying on the empowerments and key instructions of a vajra master, it is impossible for the path of mantra to dawn in one's being. Therefore, the master is essentially the same as all the buddhas, yet even kinder. For this reason, it is said that making an offering to just one pore of one's teacher's body is more beneficial than making offerings to all the buddhas throughout space and time. Hence, the first fundamental downfall, which is tremendously grave, is to feel aversion toward the master from whom one has received empowerments and key instructions of the vajra-vehicle, or to obstruct the master's intentions physically and verbally.

In general, there are a five types of teacher: (1) guides who lead you through the gateway of the doctrine, like a preceptor who gives ordination; (2) masters who elucidate the teachings and liberate one's being; (3) masters who transmit key instructions, such as a spiritual master who causes one to develop the awakened mind; (4) masters who repair one's damaged and broken vows, that is, the object for the confessions of one's nonvirtuous deeds; and (5) masters of empowerments and samayas, meaning those who grant empowerments. Other spiritual friends who have shown you kindness, even if only slightly, yet who are not one of these five are known as general masters. Of these six, common teachers should be shown the respect a sick person would show to his or her physician. The extraordinary teachers who show us the path of mantra, on the other hand, should be viewed as an actual buddha and respected as such.

Another formulation presents the following classification: (1) the general teachers who are one's virtuous spiritual friends, and (2) the guiding teachers who illuminate the doctrine of the perfections, as well as (3) teachers who bestow the empowerments of mantra, (4) teachers who explain the tantras, (5) teachers who amend degenerated and broken vows, and (6) teachers who give the key instructions. Respectively, these should be respected (1) as one's king, (2) as one's brother, (3) as one's father, (4) as one's mother, (5) as one's eyes, and (6) as even more special than one's heart. A master who transmits empowerments, explains the tantras, and grants key instructions has shown three forms of kindness and should be accorded immense respect.

3. Not Interrupting the Continuity of Mantra and Mudrā

Mantra and mūdra are symbols of enlightened speech and body, respectively. The continuity of mantra should remain uninterrupted by means of the five types of suchness. These five relate to (1) the self, (2) the deity, (3) secret mantra, (4) recitation, and (5) projection and absorption. The continuity of mūdra should remain uninterrupted by means of the four seals: (1) the great seal of visualizing the form of the deity, (2) the dharma seal of intent, (3) the samaya seal of expression, and (4) the action seal of transformation.

How should one maintain their continuity? Ideally, one maintains the continuity of the activities of mantra and mudrā during four or three daily sessions. The continuity can even be maintained with merely a single session once a day. Second best is to do four or six sessions per month. At the very least, they should be maintained once a month or once each season. One should also make offerings as much as possible; do not let years and months go by without making offerings. Should one ever feel like giving up effort in practicing the mantras and mudrās that accomplish the deity, the root samaya will degenerate.

4. Loving Those Who Have Entered the Authentic Path

Loving those who have entered the authentic path is the samaya of relatives. Until enlightenment is reached, one should never interrupt the flow of love and affection for one's companions. In general, this refers to those who follow the great vehicle, and those who follow mantra in particular. This especially refers to vajra siblings who rely on the same maṇḍala and have received empowerments and key instructions from the same master. Harboring the sincere wish to abandon these companions and other such feelings constitutes a root downfall.

In general, there are four types of relatives: (1) common relatives—all sentient beings who are brought together by a single buddha nature; (2) distant relatives—all those who have entered the teachings of the Buddha; (3) close relatives—those with similar views and conduct, and (4) inner intimate relatives—those with whom one has received empowerment. There is also a sixfold explanation that adds the following two categories: (5) the beautiful relatives—those who have the same teacher, and (6) close relatives—those who have studied the doctrine together. One should always maintain a loving attitude toward these relatives.

5. Not Explaining the Secret Meaning to Unqualified Recipients

The *Tantra of the Secret Essence* states, "Do not proclaim the secret meaning externally." Not proclaiming secrets means to speak conscientiously. It is inappropriate to explain the profound view and conduct of mantra to outsiders who are not suitable vessels, just as it is to mention such things as the faults of one's master and siblings who uphold mantra. In general, there are four secrets: (1) the profound view of mantra, (2) the deep conduct, (3) the name and form of the deity, and (4) the signs of accomplishment. These are never to be spoken of without reason. There are also four intermediate secrets that should be kept private until one completes the practice: (1) the place of practice, (2) the time of practice, (3) one's practice companions, and (4) the practice substances. The reason for keeping these secret is that not doing so may cause others to lose their faith or obstruct one's spiritual attainment. Therefore, mantric samaya substances and implements should be used in secret. One should also maintain confidentiality with respect to all that the master or one's siblings have entrusted in secrecy. From whom should all this be kept secret? It should be kept secret—by means of body, speech, and mind—from those who have damaged their samayas, those who have not received empowerment, and those without faith.

In this way, the samayas of the accomplishment of exceptional qualities involve dwelling mentally in the unexcelled meaning, reciting mantras verbally, and displaying mudrās physically. These three trainings are what one should accomplish, and their nature encompasses all trainings of mantra.

The other three root samayas assist these three trainings and guard against factors that should be avoided. For example, they reject, or guard against, going against the intentions of the master. In addition, respecting the master, the source of accomplishment, is also included in the samayas of accomplishment. Pleasing the master is also the foundation for the first two root samayas.

These five are like the root of a wish-fulfilling tree; they form the foundation for all the qualities of mantra. Since each of these five can be engaged in physically, verbally, and mentally, they are aspects of the samayas of enlightened body, speech, and mind. They can also be divided into factors that are to be guarded against and those that are to be accomplished.

2. The Ten Subsidiary Samayas

> Do not abandon delusion, attachment,
> aversion, pride or jealousy.
> The white and red nectars, the ones with odour, and human flesh,
> Are pure vessels, so do not discard them.

1. Not Abandoning the Five Poisons

The five poisons are abandoned by the listeners and purified by bodhisattvas. In mantra, however, they are brought onto the path. Because of these differences, each is superior to the last in being less deluded and more skillful. The reasons why the five poisons should not be discarded are as follows: Ultimately, there is no material substance for one to abandon, just as a dam is not needed for a mirage, while in terms of the relative, the poisons are an aid on the path when used skillfully, just as poison can be transformed into nectar. Moreover, ultimately, they are primordially enlightened as great purity and equality. This is tantamount to recognizing that someone mistakenly thought to be an enemy is, in fact, a friend. Of these three, the first and the last have already been covered.

The vehicle of the perfections also teaches how to use the poisons skillfully as an aid. Disturbing emotions may enable one to perfect the accumulations. For example, it is more valuable to offer one's body than material possessions because we harbor more attachment to the former. The poisons can also become a cause for accomplishing virtue on a vast scale. Without deliberately abandoning the disturbing emotion of desire, for instance, a bodhisattva who has not yet attained power may perfect the accumulations once he or she has taken birth due to desire. If the disturbing emotions are embraced skillfully, their identity can change into virtue. A bodhisattva who dwells on the ground of aspiring conduct may intentionally engender desire out of compassion to fulfill the hopes of a woman tormented by desire. By feeling desirous and experiencing pleasure, he then satisfies her. Because it is embraced by the skillful methods of compassion, such desire is still virtuous. This applies to other afflictive emotions as well.

There are three reasons why emotions are not discarded in the mantra vehicle: First, the five disturbing emotions are associated with the families of the thus-gone ones; second, wisdom dawns by skillfully taking them as the path; and third, they are the essence of wisdom when embraced with realization.

1. Disturbing Emotions and the Buddha Families

Attachment manifests as the mind's fervent desire for a given object. Because it has this expressive energy, at the time of the path, the mind is capable of intense longing for the qualities of the path and fruition. In the context of the fruition, it is this expressive energy that perceives all phenomena with full acceptance, without turning away from anything. With its identity that of discriminating wisdom, it is Amitābha.

Aversion manifests as the rejection of dissonant objects. The presence of this expressive energy in the mind causes the disappearance of dissonant factors in one's being in the context of the path. At the time of the fruition, this becomes mirror-like wisdom, which eliminates the stains of delusion regarding the nature of things. Thus, it is Vajra Akṣobhya, the conqueror of all obstacles and demonic forces.

Stupidity manifests as a turning away from the nature of its objects. As such, it is a condition in which one remains indifferent to a given object without giving it any thought. Since the mind has this expressive energy, it does not apprehend characteristics conceptually at the time of the path. In the context of the fruition, stupidity is identified with the wisdom of the basic space of phenomena, which does not conceive of any constructs. As such, it is Vairocana.

Pride is to feel inflated. Since the mind possesses this expressive energy, at the time of the path it is able to perform all practices without becoming discouraged, with the knowledge that there is no path superior to that of mantra. In the context of the fruition, one comes into possession of all positive qualities, so there is no sense of impoverishment or dejection and one is free from the pains of inequality at all times. As it is the wisdom of equality in essence, it is Ratnasaṃbhava.

Jealousy views oneself as unequal to another in a way that cannot be tolerated. Because the mind possesses this expressive energy, it respectively engages and turns away from what should be practiced and refrained from in the context of the path. At the time of the fruition, one is able to benefit and refrain from harming those in need of guidance. With the nature of all-accomplishing wisdom, it is Amoghasiddhi.

As with the potency of medicine and the brilliance of jewels, the mind has possessed these five self-expressive energies from the beginning. Hence, although these five perform all the activities of saṃsāra when not realized, they also perform all the pure activities of nirvāṇa once realization takes place. Thus, if one lacks the strength and energy of these five, one will be like an arrow that has lost its momentum or a machine with a broken engine; one will fail to fully accomplish the objective, just like a listener dwelling in a state of peace. Therefore, it is impossible to permanently stop the self-expressive energy of mind, and there is no need to do so either, for if they are not spoiled by delusion, the disturbing emotions manifest as the five wisdoms. The *Vimalakīrti Sūtra* explains:

> A lotus does not grow in dry ground or a desert, but from water and mud. Likewise, unsurpassable and truly perfect enlightenment does not arise from the listener's eradication of the disturbing emotions and observation of the unconditioned. Rather, the awakened mind of unsurpassable and truly perfect enlightenment arises once one develops a view of the transitory collection that is like Mount Meru. Therefore, the disturbing emotions are of the lineage of the thus-gone ones.

2. Taking Disturbing Emotions as the Path

> The world is subdued by detachment, yet accomplishment of the mudrā manifests from desire.

As this quote points out, in this world desire is considered a great fault, which is why there are teachings on how to pacify using detachment. Nevertheless, there are also occasions when desire is indispensable. According to outer mantra, unless a person with samayas harbors mental desire for the mudrā, which is explained to be the symbolic deity, no accomplishments will be attained. According to inner mantra, unless one has intense desire for his or her spiritual partner, wisdom and accomplishment will not be attained. Consequently, it is taught that one will not achieve the spiritual attainments of the mudrās if desire is lacking.

Hence, the more desire one has, such as the workable faculty endowed with the desire of the desire realm, the more bliss there will be. The more one skillfully embraces bliss, the more powerful the vision of wisdom becomes, just like fuel causing a fire to blaze and poison increasing a peacock's luster. Likewise, the other disturbing emotions will also function as conditions for either faults or positive qualities depending on whether or not they are skillfully utilized. Nevertheless, the essence of these conditions remains the same.

It is indeed taught that wishing for a defiled object is desire, whereas aspiring to the qualities of complete purification is not. Nevertheless, the function of desire in these two instances differs merely in terms of its objects, features, and so forth. Both forms of desire are identical in the way that the expressive energy of the mind moves toward an object. This is also taught in the sūtras. The *Sūtra Requested by Sāgaramati* explains:

> The more hay is put on fire,
> The stronger and larger it becomes.
> The more disturbing emotions a bodhisattva has,
> The stronger the fire of wisdom will blaze.

3. Disturbing Emotions as the Essence of Wisdom

For someone who apprehends all appearances to be ordinary and who, thereby, perceives them as real selves and phenomena, the expressive energy of mind will arise as the five poisons. However, all phenomena are actually pure; their nature cannot be established as either a self or phenomena. As this is the case, they are equality and free from all reference points.

When this is seen, the five expressive energies of awareness will dawn as wisdom. For example, when a beautiful object is seen, ordinary people will cling to subject and object and feel attachment. Those practicing ascetic discipline will counteract this attachment by meditating on repulsiveness and other such remedies. In the present context, however, any thought that manifests is allowed to arise without being suppressed. When embraced by a mind that realizes reality, the appearances of subject and object, as well as the experience of bliss, are unobstructed and there is an experience of unimpeded openness free from reference points. As the object is clearly experienced, directly and intensely, in the form of bliss, this is desire manifesting as discriminating wisdom. This can also be applied to the rest of the disturbing emotions.

Hence, it is only in mantra that one finds these instructions for taking disturbing emotions as the path. The sūtras merely teach their nature. The *Sūtra of the Mudrā for Engaging in the Generation of the Power of Faith*, for example, states:

> There is no wisdom apart from the nature of disturbing emotions.
> The very nature of disturbing emotions is wisdom.

2. Not Discarding the Five Nectars
The five things that should not be discarded are the five nectars that one should not abandon. They are not to be discarded because the polarity of pure/impure does not exist from the perspective of equality. Moreover, since these nectars are pure, they should be readily accepted. Conduct that transcends notions of clean and dirty allows one to experience equality and overpower conceptual thoughts. Through disciplined conduct, moreover, one will quickly attain the spiritual attainments. When these entities are skillfully embraced, they turn into worldly nectar. Also, since the five nectars are essentially substances of accomplishment, they should be readily accepted.

Since observing the command brings about spiritual attainments, the periodic offerings of nectar should not be interrupted. If one engages in such forms of conduct in a distorted manner without having realized the profound nature, they are vulgar and detrimental to one's own being. On the other hand, when one's realization is perfected, there is no need to deliberately engage in such acts. Thus, the five nectars should be utilized as aides in various ways according to one's experience of realization, just as those who learn the art of swordsmanship practice with wood and lead before using an actual sword.

Without these ten subsidiary samayas, one will be unable to fully engage in this extraordinary, quick, and easy path, which involves taking the five poisons as the path and other such practices. By fully engaging in this path, however, the disturbing emotions themselves manifest as wisdom. When that happens, the truth of origin is the essence of the truth of the path, and suffering is the embodiment of enlightenment when the ripened aggregates themselves dawn as the wisdom of purity. Hence, this path is extremely powerful. With these subsidiary samayas, the profound conduct of mantra is spontaneously present in one's being.

When divided extensively, there are three hundred and sixty root and subsidiary samayas, as elucidated in other scriptures. In brief, however, when it comes to achieving buddhahood, not transgressing the view of great purity and equality is the king of all samayas. Nevertheless, since these vows correspond to the mind-sets of sentient beings, the various samayas that either directly or indirectly have an impact on this process are limitless.

3. The Principles of the Key Points of Samaya

Without a single exception, all the disciplines and vows of individual liberation and the awakened mind are included in the samayas of the mantra vehicle of great skillful methods. When contrasted with the conduct of the lower vehicles, the samayas of mantra are exceedingly pure. It should, moreover, go without saying that forms of conduct shared by these approaches do not conflict since even those that appear to contradict the ethical principles of lower systems are not in conflict, but are far superior.

For example, in the context of individual liberation, four principles are taught that may cause a root infraction: the complete presence of object, intention, application, and completion. Even so, while the vows of individual liberation specify that one must merely avoid harming others, the bodhisattva vow adds to this, mandating that one must also benefit others. Therefore, when bodhisattvas have a compassionate intention that is undefiled by self-interest, engaging in sexual relations and other such actions are not problematic. In fact, such acts are virtuous. Actions motivated by self-interest, however, such as praising oneself, disparaging others, and not teaching the doctrine or not giving away one's wealth due to stinginess, are said to be infractions.

In the mantra vehicle, one gains confidence in the view of equality, whereby neither subject nor object are observed. Therefore, the apparent act of killing and other such activities are entirely devoid of ordinary objects, intentions, application, and completion. Since they involve wisdom and skillful means, they are extraordinary ways to accomplish the twofold benefit, albeit merely in terms of the relative. Thus, since one is untainted by faults, the vows of individual liberation are complete and included in the samayas. Because one acts altruistically, moreover, the same holds for the vows of the awakened mind. The latter builds upon the value of the former, like the gradual progression of iron, silver, and gold.

Furthermore, when a copper vessel is used as a bed-pan, it is dirty; when it is used as a wash basin, it is clean; when it is used as an implement for offerings to the deities, it is extremely clean; and when it is used to make a statue of a buddha, it is an object of veneration. Likewise, if the activities of one's body, speech, and mind manifest in tandem with disturbing emotions, they will bind one to saṃsāra. When partially embraced by knowledge and method, however, one will turn away from actions that should be avoided, and those that are acted out will cause happiness and liberation. Acts that are embraced by great methods and knowledge, moreover, will become causes for unexcelled awakening, and when embraced by tremendously great methods and knowledge, they will cause the effortless and spontaneously present great enlightenment. Therefore, due to this process of transformation, the higher vows are much purer than the lower ones.

To summarize, in sexual intercourse, for example, ordinary people are motivated by a desire for the bliss that comes from the joining of the male and female organs. This, in turn, causes them to fixate on the bliss of ejaculation that occurs during the act itself. When the act is concluded, the seed of desire is sown in the mind, thus binding the individual to saṃsāra.

Practitioners, on the other hand, are motivated by the aspiration for undefiled great bliss and other such principles. Preparing the cause for great merit in this way, they then allow ordinary desire to dawn as the wisdom of bliss as the actual practice. This is brought about through (1) the power of the blessings of the mudrās of enlightened body, speech, and mind, (2) the strength of the method of key instructions for binding the energies and mind within the central channel, and (3) the ability of knowledge to move toward wisdom. At the conclusion of this process, the ordinary mind and all its habitual tendencies are incinerated like a thicket by fire-like wisdom. In this way, the conduct of mantra can be proven to be superior to that of other approaches. This can be applied to other contexts as well.

In this way, the purity of conduct is established through the power of wisdom. Wisdom arises from, or is the essence of, the pure view. Therefore, one should know that the life force of the samayas is upheld by the view. The *Awesome Flash of Lightning* says:

> Thus, what is referred to as "samaya"
> Is said to be one's own view.

4. Purpose
This section contains a general explanation and a specific discussion of seven qualities.

The General Purpose
The samayas are like wish-fulfilling jewels in being the source of all that is needed. They are like the life force of all virtuous faculties. Whoever transgresses them will be wasting all the practices of mantra, in the same way that a broken vessel is unable to hold any liquid. In this way, since the samayas are like the ground in being the basis for all positive qualities, they are an indispensable basis for accomplishing the dharma-kingdom of great beings.

The Specific Purpose
Having these samayas will enable one to obtain limitless sublime qualities. In the system of the general vehicles, one speaks of "view, conduct, and accompaniments," which refers to the three trainings in wisdom, absorption, and discipline. In terms of discipline, higher forms of discipline are superior to lower ones, and there are innumerable ways in which the vows of the bodhisattva vehicle are more exalted than the vows of individual liberation. In short, just as there are seven qualities that set the great vehicle apart, including its vast scope, the vows that assist this approach are correspondingly superior.

It is hard to fathom the depths of the great vehicle, insofar as it is profound and vast, accomplishes the twofold benefit, does not contradict the twofold selflessness, and so on. While this may be the case, due to their profound and vast qualities, the samayas of mantra are superior to the vows of the bodhisattvas in limitless ways. The *Tantra of the Secret Essence*, however, condenses these into seven superior qualities with the verses that begin, "Moreover, the supreme king, Samantabhadra's seal . . ." First, these qualities are spontaneously present and need no cultivation because they are marked with the seal of Samantabhadra. The listeners are born merely through the teachings of the Buddha; they do not belong to the family of the Buddha. Consequently, they are not marked by the seal of the Buddha, but merely by the seal of blessings. Since bodhisattvas belong to the family of the Buddha, they are stamped by the seal of the Buddha. Nevertheless, they are not marked by the seal of spontaneous presence because they maintain that buddhahood is newly accomplished. However, according to the approach of unsurpassable mantra, all phenomena are in a state of full enlightenment as the maṇḍalas of enlightened body, speech, and mind. Thus, they are said to be stamped with the seal of Samantabhadra. That being so, the fruition and all its marvelous qualities are spontaneously and effortlessly present.

Second, the power of blessings is superior in this approach because those who practice it are viewed as sacred objects of veneration by the chief of the world and his retinue. The listeners are venerated by Brahma, Śiva, Indra, and other gods, yet they are not as esteemed as the bodhisattvas. The bodhisattvas, in turn, are not venerated as highly as the buddhas. However, those who hold vows and engage in the sphere of buddha activity are accorded respect on par with the great veneration received by the buddhas themselves. Therefore, those who possess the samayas of mantra and engage in the sphere of buddha activity are venerated like crown-jewels by the dharma-protecting guardians who obey their commands as they would a buddha's. These beings include the great worldly gods and the mother deities and ḍākinīs that make up their retinues. Consequently, the strength of their supportive companions makes such individuals extremely powerful.

Third, since the buddhas and bodhisattvas consider such individuals their children or relatives, blessings occur swiftly. In the same way that a qualified son of a universal monarch is sure to ascend to the royal throne, a knowledge holder who is in accord with the realization and deeds of the Buddha himself is regarded as "one who upholds the lineage of the thus-gone ones." Like a reflection appearing in a clear pond, pure view and meditation enable blessings to quickly enter the being of those who are aided by the potency of the samayas.

Fourth, since the experiential domains of such individuals accord with that of the thus-gone ones, the experiential domains in this approach are particularly exalted. While a practitioner of secret mantra experiences the nature of the primordial state of purity and equality without accepting or rejecting, buddha activity remains uninterrupted. For this reason, the experiential domains of such a practitioner accord with that of the thus-gone ones. This is not the case with the other two vows, which relate to the systems of the noble foe destroyers and bodhisattvas who dwell on the great grounds. Consequently, the experiential domains of the samayas of mantra are particularly exalted.

Fifth, because all phenomena are joined with the field of Samantabhadra, there is no fear and anxiety. Since all saṃsāric phenomena dwell primordially in a state of great purity and equality, there is nothing to accept or reject; this is the field of Samantabhadra. Whoever realizes this will dwell in a state in which all the anxieties of saṃsāra that are caused by disturbing emotions and suffering, as well as any fears of falling from the path, have been eliminated.

When dreaming of being swept away by a river, those who recognize that they are dreaming are not scared. Aware that these appearances will disappear once they wake up, they will do their best to awake from their sleep. Likewise, here saṃsāra and nirvāṇa are not viewed as something to abandon and a remedy, respectively. Therefore, there is no need to strive on a path that necessitates discarding the disturbing emotions. Instead, one simply rests without straying from the great mindfulness that embraces disturbing emotions with the supreme wisdom of realizing their nature.

Sixth, whether one teaches the vows of the provisional or definitive meaning, all are subject to the principles of natural spontaneous presence and complete purity, as was taught previously.

Seventh, even if damaged, the samayas can be restored by being amended. Listeners believe that phenomena are real entities and that physical and verbal actions are the most significant entities. Therefore, like a broken clay pot, their vows cannot be repaired once damaged. Bodhisattvas do not believe that phenomena are real entities. They teach the primacy of mind. Accordingly, any breaches of their vows can be completely restored by relying on a spiritual friend, in the same way that a skilled goldsmith can repair a broken golden vase such that it becomes even better than its former state. In the mantra vehicle, the primary factors are held to be the realization of great purity and equality and the mastery in awareness of the illusory display. For this reason, any breach of its vows can be naturally restored without relying on any other support, just as a dented gold or silver vessel can be repaired through one's own efforts when no goldsmith is available.

These seven qualities of the mantra samayas can be expanded upon to an infinite degree. Alternatively, these qualities can also be condensed into five categories, since the first quality is the inconceivable samaya of the inconceivable reality, while the fourth and fifth qualities can be combined into one category as the principles of essence and function.

In short, the samayas are not to be transgressed. In other words, samayas involve not wavering from the view, dwelling in the maṇḍala, maintaining the meaning of the empowerment in one's being, and not transgressing the meditation, conduct, accomplishment, offering, enlightened activity, mantra, and mudrā. Putting an end to factors that conflict with these vows constitutes the prohibitive, or guarded, samaya. The samaya is universally pervasive and is the essential way to abide by the path of mantra without transgression. It is, therefore, the embodiment of the deity and the way of vajra mantra.

In terms of the final meaning, since all phenomena are great purity and equality from the very beginning, one should know that the culmination of the natural great perfection, in which there is no affirming, negating, accepting, or rejecting, is absence, openness, spontaneous presence, and oneness. The *Tantra of the Secret Essence* states:

> If one abides by the samaya of equality,
> Which unites equally with equality,
> One will attain the great perfection of equality.
> Thus, if transgressed, there will be no buddhahood.

This concludes the teaching on samayas, the perfection of discipline.

7. Accomplishment

Accomplishment will be presented in terms of its (1) essence, (2) divisions, (3) principle, and (4) purpose.

1. Essence

> By practicing free from doubt
> With the absence of laziness and sloth,
> All maṇḍalas will be accomplished
> And the sacred and supreme vajra secret attained.

And also:

> Approach and close approach,
> Accomplishment and great accomplishment...

The term *sādhana* means "to take up fully." Since it allows one to take up and attain one's desired objective, or accomplish it, it is called "accomplishment." Alternatively, the term "accomplishment" can be said to derive from the word *siddhi*. By virtue of the various levels of spiritual attainment that are to be accomplished, these attainments and their accomplishment are referred to as "spiritual attainments." In actuality, all the practices that employ the unique methods of secret mantra to accomplish the common and supreme spiritual attainments that one desires and strives toward are subsumed within the two divisions of approach and accomplishment.

2. Divisions
This section consists of a general explanation and a specific explanation of the unique group accomplishment.

1. General Explanation
The general presentation itself has four sections. First, both the common and supreme spiritual attainments are what are accomplished. The common spiritual attainments are further divided into minor and major acts, while the supreme spiritual attainments are classified as either temporary or ultimate. Furthermore, practices such as resurrections, longevity practices, and mirror-divinations are meant to accomplish the common spiritual attainments, while Vajrasattva, group accomplishment, medicinal accomplishment, and other such practices are meant to accomplish the supreme spiritual attainments.

Second, when divided in terms of support, there are four categories: the substances of the various outer implements, and, internally, verbal mantra recitation, mental meditative concentration, and physical actions, such as particular gazes. Spiritual attainments are gained by utilizing these supports. There can also be twofold, threefold, or fourfold divisions, as well as limitless subdivisions within each individual category. Although accomplishments based on mere substances, such as the accomplishment of minor activities, are indeed accomplishments, they are not genuine accomplishments. Genuine accomplishment, which is the accomplishment mentioned as one of the eleven topics, is an exceptional method that enables one to attain the ultimate fruition swiftly and easily. Nevertheless, when embraced by special methods and knowledge, such as compassion, even lesser activities become part of the genuine path. Since they may be necessary temporarily, there is nothing wrong in accomplishing them.

One may wonder what the difference is between enlightened activity and accomplishment. Although enlightened activity can indeed be grouped under accomplishment, these two are dissimilar in the sense that accomplishment is method while activity is the fruition of method. Likewise, although both of these are generally categorized as conduct, there is a difference in terms of the degree of specificity and other such factors. One should, therefore, know how these principles are included in other categories and divided.

Third are divisions in terms of the essence of accomplishment. This refers to accomplishment based on the development and completion stage, respectively.

Fourth are divisions in terms of the principle of accomplishment. This can refer to either approach and accomplishment or, if these are divided further in terms of cause and effect, the four branches of approach, close approach, accomplishment, and great accomplishment.

2. Group Accomplishment

The reason this is called "exceptional accomplishment" is because its cause, essence, and fruition are superior. Its cause is superior because of the blessings it generates for attaining spiritual attainments due to the power of all the outer implements and, internally, the assembly of male and female practitioners who have attained ability, all coming together at the same time. Its essence is superior because of the ability to attain the fruition without any obstacles. This, in turn, is due to the continuous effort that is directed toward the four branches of approach and accomplishment. Finally, its fruition is superior insofar as one attains the undefiled state of a knowledge holder.

With this form of group accomplishment, the basis of accomplishment is maintained via the five perfections. The scriptures are then followed through the four branches of approach and accomplishment. As a result, the fruition, the state of the four knowledge holders, is quickly accomplished in thirty-six days or some such period. The five perfections are the perfect place, time, teacher, retinue, and substance. The perfect place means any auspicious place that is found to be good and free from obstacles when investigated. The perfect time refers to the period when the time has come for the practitioners to engage in group accomplishment. It begins on an auspicious day with the proper date and astrological features and lasts until the activities of the great accomplishment have been completed. The perfect teacher is a master who is learned in the profound scriptures of secret mantra, has gained power in their meaning, and, for these reasons, is worthy to be a vajra king. The perfect retinue consists of the regent, wife, skeleton dancers, karma, eyes, sweeper, and so on, each with their respective qualities. This retinue is equal in number to the deities accomplished in the gathering of the male and female practitioners who are worthy to assemble in the profound maṇḍala. The perfect substance consists of the coming together of the complete range of edible sustenance, illness-averting medicines, necessary implements, and substances for accomplishment.

When these five perfections are present, one can practice the profound accomplishment via the four aspects of approach and accomplishment. First, one practices by pleasing the deity for the approach. Following this, one becomes genuinely oriented toward attaining the spiritual attainments for the close approach, and then gains the spiritual accomplishments through accomplishment. Great accomplishment refers to the full accomplishment that occurs once the spiritual attainments have been acquired.

To dispel adverse conditions, one should set the outer boundary and subdue samaya breakers. The inner boundary can then be set and the maṇḍala erected. The preliminary practices consist of the five preparations. Respectively, these five relate to the maṇḍala, deities, master, substances, and students. For the main part of the practice, one first draws the maṇḍala image on a place that has been blessed as the interior of the liberated *matraṃ*. Then the substances for accomplishment are arranged there and, together with the rest, all the implements are blessed in the correct manner. For the conclusion, the maṇḍala recitation is performed, various offerings are made, the maṇḍala is entered, and one receives empowerment. Everything up until this point constitutes the *approach*.

Next, by correctly following the practice text and putting effort into recitation and meditation, one will see the signs of accomplishment getting closer. This is the *close approach* to the deity.

Accomplishment consists of actualizing stable signs of accomplishment through practice. If the deity is peaceful, one transforms it into a wrathful deity or one visualizes the deity's radiation and absorption, regardless of whether the basis for accomplishment is peaceful or wrathful. Effort is placed on recitation, while food, drinks, ornaments, garments, and all other desirable things are enjoyed as the play of empty bliss. The deities are also pleased with dance and mudrās. Through this practice, the stable signs of spiritual attainment are actualized. This is *accomplishment*.

Great accomplishment occurs when the spiritual attainments are acquired. In one night, between dusk and dawn, one gains the spiritual attainments of the enlightened body, speech, and mind of the maṇḍala. At dusk, one should practice radiation and absorption and acquire accomplishments from the deities, whereas one should practice liberation and take accomplishments from the enemy at midnight. At dawn, one should practice union and take accomplishments from one's consort.

Utilizing this form of group practice will gradually induce the symbolic and actual wisdoms and one will come to dwell on the level of a noble one. Previously attained forms of realization will gradually develop until the unified state of nonlearning has been reached. This, in turn, will enable one to attain the levels of the four knowledge holders.

3. Principle

This explanation has two parts: (1) how to achieve accomplishment, and (2) the fruition of this accomplishment.

1. How to Achieve Accomplishment

This section is divided further into two parts: (1) the development stage and (2) the completion stage. In the development stage, one begins by resting one's attention on a focal support, such as a buddha statue placed before oneself. By familiarizing oneself with this process, one will progress through the five meditation experiences. This, in turn, will enable one to attain accomplishment by becoming proficient in the practice of appearance and existence being divine form. Here, having sharp faculties, observing the samayas, and training in the key instructions constitute the aspect of approach, meditating one-pointedly on the divine form is close approach, gaining stability is accomplishment, and perfecting the practice is great accomplishment.

There are two variations of the completion stage, one with signs and one without signs. The former is method, while the latter is the outcome of this method. In the completion stage with signs, which constitutes approach, one uses the support of one's own body to produce an experience of empty bliss using the subtle essences, energetic practices, and inner heat. In the completion stage without signs, which is accomplishment, one utilizes the support of another's body and actualizes co-emergent joy through the practices of descent, retention, reversal, and pervasion. Since each of these can also be divided in terms of method and the outcome of method, these two encompass the four aspects of approach and accomplishment.

Using the method of one's own body also constitutes the four branches of approach and accomplishment, insofar as it involves the stages of receiving key instructions, putting them into practice, stabilizing the practice, and bringing it to perfection. As for utilizing another's body, approach involves knowing the key instructions, attracting a knowledge consort, and so forth. Close approach is the union of the vajra and lotus that follows consecration. Accomplishment is the arousal of the first three joys. Great accomplishment is the experience of co-emergent joy. In addition, the four joys themselves are also the four aspects of approach and accomplishment from the perspective of the former stages causing the latter ones, which are their effects.

In short, these four branches of approach and accomplishment are divided into the path of actual accomplishment and the preceding cause, regardless of which spiritual attainment one is trying to attain. One may then make further internal divisions in terms of cause and effect. Consequently, these four stages encompass the five paths in their entirety. One should be aware that these four can also be correlated with other factors, even down to a single practice session.

As for the completion stage without features, all conceptual paths are really nothing more than methods for realizing the luminous great perfection without features. Thus, when practitioners with a gradual inclination meditate on the methods presented in these paths, they will be able to access this primordial stage. On the other hand, students with sharp faculties who are suited for the instantaneous approach of the great perfection will not need to rely on blissful melting and other such methods. Instead, they will be able to enter this state merely by the power of the master's key instructions and the transference of blessings. In either case, this is the sacred fruition of all other completion stage practices.

Moreover, the master's key instructions enable one to recognize, directly and nakedly, that the nature of one's own mind is empty yet aware, that it is self-occurring wisdom, innately free from constructs. With this recognition, one comes to rest in a state without accepting or rejecting and without artifice or fabrication. In this regard, approach is to receive the key instructions that point out this state. Since this stage is the gateway to the natural and spontaneously present great maṇḍala, it is likened to opening one's eyes. Close approach involves understanding the nature. This stage is likened to actually seeing the maṇḍala. Accomplishment refers to training in accord with this understanding, thus bringing forth an experience of one's indwelling wisdom, which is likened to entering the maṇḍala. Great accomplishment involves gaining certainty in the nature of the great perfection, which occurs once one's training is stable and any clinging to the efforts of the path and the claims of the philosophical positions of the eight vehicles have collapsed. This stage is likened to becoming empowered into the maṇḍala.

It is, therefore, impossible to enter this natural great maṇḍala using attributes and material substances. Rather, it can be accessed only through the strength of self-awareness. To rest in that state without contrivance is the method for settling the mind. Out of this state, the wisdom that beholds the uncontrived nature will dawn as natural luminosity. This is the path of the great perfection, the fruition of the method for placing the mind.

2. The Fruition of Accomplishment

There are three points that describe how wisdom unfolds once one has practiced this path: (1) the wisdom of appearance, (2) the wisdom of emptiness, and (3) the wisdom of unity. In the experience of a practitioner of the development stage, the wisdom of appearance refers to the appearance of the created form of the deity. For a practitioner of the completion stage, it refers to the divine forms and other limitless appearances that manifest within the state of luminosity. Such manifestations are mere products of the energetic mind and appear only as a self-display (as illustrated by the twelve examples of illusion).

With the wisdom of emptiness, one dissolves the deity's appearance once a stable absorption in the development stage has been achieved and contemplates without maintaining a mental reference point. Practitioners of the completion stage experience the fourfold emptiness based on practices that involve conceptual methods. During the last emptiness, co-emergent luminosity is seen.

The wisdom of unity refers to the natural state of all phenomena, the unity of basic space and awareness. When this unity is experienced as natural luminosity within the nature of one's mind—naturally and without contrivance—one dwells in the great perfection, free from fabricated visualizations and methods that require conscious effort.

These three wisdoms are also posited in relation to the realization of the natural state of purity, equality, and indivisibility, respectively. However, in essence, the illusory body appears as emptiness; luminosity is one's unobstructed self-display; and, as such, these two are a unity. They are taught in this manner because of their varying degrees of emphasis.

Likewise, while each expresses its own unique qualities when presented together, the terms "purity" and "equality" can each be used to demonstrate both principles. The term "purity" demonstrates the relative purity of the deity and that the ultimate is purified of conceptual activity. "Equality" demonstrates the relative indivisible equality of buddhas and sentient beings, and the ultimate equality of the basic space free from constructs. In this way, one should be aware that both of these terms have the ability to illustrate the meaning of primordial enlightenment. This is widely taught throughout the tantras.

With each of these three wisdoms, such as the illusory body, one may distinguish between experience and realization. Experiences, moreover, can also be classified as being stable, unstable, and so forth. There are other ways of categorizing as well. They can be correlated with each of the four modes, for example: (1) the literal meaning in accord with the perfection vehicle, (2) the general meaning in accord with the development stage, (3) the hidden meaning in accord with the completion stage with signs, and (4) the ultimate meaning in accord with the great perfection without signs, or the fruition. Each of these four modes is superior to those that precede it, yet all are oriented toward the ultimate meaning.

Training exclusively in meditative absorption on the path of the subtle essence and so forth can induce the experience of the fourfold emptiness. This occurs in a way that broadly resembles the manner in which luminosity is sustained in relation to union, deep sleep, and dying. However, the way in which the subtle movement of the energetic mind ceases is very different. Until the subtle energetic mind has been dissolved there can be no ultimate luminosity.

The expanse of luminosity, in which the entirety of the eighty natural concepts together with their mounts have dissolved, has the identity of the unceasing clarity of awareness. Of the twofold division of mind and wisdom, this expanse is wisdom, not mind, because it is the clarity of nondual awareness, which is of one taste with basic space. It is reality, not phenomena, because it is the inexpressible unity of appearance and emptiness—the nature of mind. Although there is a great deal that can be said in this context, it shall be explained elsewhere.

As this principle is even taught in the vehicle of the perfections, it is also part of the vajra vehicle. The *Sūtra Requested by Sāgaramati* states:

> How can space become afflicted?
> It is possible that this may be shown in the future,
> But the natural luminous clarity of the perfectly awakened mind
> Can never become afflicted.

While the *Ornament of the Mahāyāna Sūtras* explains:

> Mind is said to be naturally luminous at all times,
> But made unwholesome by transitory faults.
> Any mind that is different from the mind of reality,
> Is not luminosity, which is said to be natural.

And the *Unexcelled Continuity* says:

> The nature of mind is luminous,
> And unchanging like space.
> Although desire and the rest appear from incorrect concepts,
> It remains undisturbed by these temporary stains.

In this context, unless one genuinely understands the nature of the ground to be the unity of the indivisible truths, one will not be able to fully ascertain the ground luminosity. If "luminosity" were a mere vacant absence, the mind would perish when all minds and mental states recede. Even if luminosity were empty like space, who could recognize this in the absence of a mind? Similarly, if luminosity is understood to be merely the clarity and awareness of an ordinary mind, and if it is said to be found even in dualistic investigation and analysis, then why would luminosity not be found within in the other eighty natural concepts as well?

Therefore, the mind's natural state is a primordial unity of inseparable basic space and awareness. It is beyond comprehension by dualistic concepts. Like primordial space, it dwells without transition or change. By the power of the path, it is experienced as a nondual self-clarity by the wisdom that arises from the self-expression of reality itself. This is known as beholding luminosity.

If one does not part from the self-expression of wisdom, there will be neither confusion nor liberation; one will simply dwell in the ground. However, when distracting circumstances cause one to stray from this self-expression, one will be in discord with the ground and give rise to dualistic perception. This is what we call "mind." This confusion is the repository for all the habitual tendencies of saṃsāra, like a storage container. When this self-expression manifests undistortedly, it is called "wisdom." Wisdom is like a fire that burns the thicket of duality and the predispositions for saṃsāra, bringing liberation. It is very important not to confuse the essential points of these two.

The scriptures of the great perfection demonstrate with great clarity the difference between consciousness and wisdom. The *Sūtra of Descent into Lanka* also speaks of this:

> Mind performs actions and so on,
> While wisdom is what distinguishes.

The *King of Absorption* says:

> Through knowing the nature of mind,
> Wisdom arises again.

Consciousness and wisdom are similar in terms of merely being aware and knowing. However, they differ insofar as one is a mistaken apprehension that fails to correctly comprehend its object, while the other is an unmistaken awareness of the object as it is. It must be understood that wisdom remains even once dualistic consciousness is overcome.

In terms of the ground, as a sentient being, these two are like ice and water. Although confusion may take place, it does so within a state of luminosity. And though one may be liberated at a later point in time, this liberation also occurs within luminosity. This is an extremely important point to understand. The *Wheel of Time* states:

> In the treatises of non-Buddhists, that which is not the awareness of reality is referred to as *"awareness."* What is awareness? It *is* the emptiness of *inner-awareness* and *unchanging* bliss *also*. These were *fully stated in this world by the sages*. What is it? Unchanging luminosity is *that which appears as the entirety of the three worlds*, and *lo, lord of humans, that into which it dissolves again.*

In this way, wisdom is situated within the ground. However, since the basic space of phenomena is the union of appearance and emptiness, it is not simply a mere empty state; it possesses the quality of clear awareness. In essence, it is beyond confusion and liberation. Hence, it is classified as such simply because it does not stray from this state. Nevertheless, it is very important not to mistake this for liberated wisdom—the wisdom that arises from the display of the ground once one has genuinely realized it for what it is.

Moreover, one should understand that it is only in the scriptures of the great perfection that one will find clear explanations of the way ground manifestations arise from the ground, the way confusion and liberation appear from that, and the way in which it is impossible to become confused again once confusion has been reversed within the ground. A general explanation of this topic was also offered above in the chapter on the ground.

In this way, the mantras and mudrās that are the primary elements of the development and completion stages, as well as all the other areas of training in secret mantra, are brought together. By assembling all facets of the path that are called for, both temporary and ultimate objectives are accomplished quickly and with ease, like a magical apparition. This is "the accomplishment of secret mantra."

4. Purpose

Accomplishment is extremely significant since the attainment of all desired objects, whether of a temporary or ultimate nature, depends on it. In brief, accomplishment is what actualizes the meaning that was ascertained via the view and enables one to capture the ultimate and lasting dominion. Moreover, diligent conduct that employs maṇḍala, absorption, samayas, empowerment, offerings, mantra, and mudrā will allow one to gain spiritual attainments. Thereby, one will engage in manifold enlightened activities for the sake of others, fulfilling their wishes in the process. In this way, accomplishment encompasses all the other aspects of training as well.

In the final analysis, all accomplishment and its objects are a mere self-display. Therefore, in the sense that one's own mind has been buddha from the very beginning, there is nothing to accomplish. Resting in the state of spontaneously present equality and perfection with an understanding of this point is the perfection of accomplishment. On this topic, the *Tantra of the Secret Essence* says:

In all the ten directions and four times,
The perfect buddha will not be found.
Mind itself is the perfect buddha.
Do not search for the buddha elsewhere.

This concludes the teaching on the topic of accomplishment, the perfection of diligence.

8. Offerings
Offerings are discussed in terms of their (1) essence, (2) divisions, (3) principle, and (4) purpose.

1. Essence

Through a difference in clarity, fortunate ones
Unite with the basic space of phenomena,

Either gradually or instantaneously,
And meditate on the great offering mudrā.

The Sanskrit term *pūja* means "to generate before," "to repeatedly generate joy," or "to revere." Thus, offerings precede any virtuous activity and are produced prior to pleasing the deities and before any activity is performed. Alternatively, in terms of reverence, offerings are meant to continuously please. To elaborate, in terms of identity, offerings are actions that please by means of the various inner and outer things that are presented with an intention to physically, verbally, and mentally worship and revere the recipient of the offerings.

2. Divisions
This section has two parts: (1) the unique specific divisions and (2) an explanation of the common gathering circle.

1. The Unique Specific Divisions
Generally, offerings are divided in terms of being either worldly or transcendent, surpassed or unsurpassed, or presented in actuality or imagined. Other distinctions can also be made in terms of common and unique offerings, and

with regard to the recipient, intention, and substances that are offered. In terms of support, there is an inner classification in terms of the continuum of body, speech, and mind and an outer classification that consists of substances and implements. In terms of the form of offering, there is also a threefold division into service, material offerings, and practice. There are also outer, common offerings, which are the offerings that are worthy as pleasing gifts in the world. These well-known offerings are mentioned in the outer tantras of mantra. The inner, special offerings are unique to inner mantra and are included within the offering substances, support substances, amendment substances, and accomplishment substances. The secret, marvelous offering is to offer the five poisons as the five wisdoms. The offering of appearance and existence as great bliss is made by undertaking activity, such as union and liberation, by means of the view of great purity and equality, the meditation of appearance and existence manifesting as the ground, and the conduct of self-liberating whatever arises.

All these distinctions can also be condensed in terms of their essential character into four categories: (1) the outer offering of enjoyments, (2) the inner offering of sacred substances, (3) the secret offering of union and liberation, and (4) the suchness offering of great equality. The outer offering consists of seven offerings: (1) mudrā dances, (2) songs of praise, (3) an absorbed mind, (4) various pleasant objects, (5) marvelous specific substances, (6) supreme methods, and (7) appearance and existence as manifest ground. The mudrā dance encompasses many types of mudrā, such as dances with the feet, gestures with the hands, gazes with the eyes, postures of the body, and expressions of dance. Songs of praise have several melodies, such as the *shatapa*. In terms of words, there are many, such as those that evoke commitments, eulogies, supplications, those that bring joy, and mantra words of offering. In making offerings through absorption, one first develops faith and devotion and then emanates infinite offering clouds via meditative concentration. At the same time, through wisdom one understands that they are without intrinsic existence. The offering of pleasant objects refers to the seven desired objects, the six sense pleasures, and in particular one's clothes, jewelry, food, drinks, belongings, dwelling place, domain, and wealth. Marvelous specific substances are the individual unique offering substances and supportive substances of the deities and protectors as they are described in the scriptures. Offering by supreme methods refers to the fire offering and other such rituals. To make offerings based on fire is a method that uniquely satisfies the deities. As such, it is more exalted than other offerings. Likewise, with the thread-cross of offering and appeasement and other methods, one can accomplish many great goals with little hardship. Finally, offering appearance and existence as the manifest ground means to mentally make an offering of all the phenomena that appear and exist as a single whole. This resembles the offering of pure realms found in the common vehicles. In this context, however, since the world and its inhabitants dwell primordially as the great bliss of purity and equality along with all pure and impure phenomena, everything within appearance and existence is offered in the form of an offering of empty bliss. This is also termed "the offering of appearance and existence as manifest ground" and "the offering that is indivisible with the ever-excellent."

The inner offering of sacred substances is explicitly taught to be the sacred substance of nectar, the great red rakta, and the baliṅ torma. Moreover, it can also refer to the elements of the channels, energies, and essences in the vajra body, manifesting as various pure offerings.

The secret offering is explicitly taught to be union and liberation. This also refers to offering the five poisons as the five wisdoms, the three poisons as enlightened body, speech, and mind, and so on.

The offering of suchness is to acknowledge natural equality within the single sphere of the dharma body. Here, the great bliss of the purity and equality of appearance and existence is offered, without focusing on an offering, recipient, and an act of offering. This is the king of all offerings that delight the thus-gone ones.

The outer offerings and the rest of the four offerings are connected with the four empowerments and their corresponding views, meditations, and samayas. In this way, there are limitless subdivisions of offerings, which is why the individual classes of tantra speak of such a diversity of offerings. The *Tantra of the Secret Essence*, however, explicitly mentions offerings only in terms of substances, fire ritual, meditative absorption, union and liberation, nectar, and songs of praise. According to the key instructions of masters of the past, there are fourteen offerings related to the peaceful and wrathful deities. These are mentioned in the following lines:

> Respectful homage, mudrā dance,
> Samantabhadra, cooling water, four crossings,
> Nectar, torma, beverages,
> Superior meditative absorption, union, liberation,
> Pleasing objects, wisdom music, and wisdom songs.

The offerings for wrathful deities are similar, except the offering of raising the rakta three times is used instead of the offering of superior meditative absorption.

2. The Common Gathering Circle

This topic involves three explanations: (1) how it is common, (2) its purpose, and (3) the way to perform it. Why is this gathering circle referred to as "common"? The reason for describing it as common is that it contains all the offerings that are taught within the outer, inner, secret, and suchness offerings. The gathering offering is deeply significant because it is the highest form of offering and not just a limited offering ritual. As is said, "a gathering offering is the highest form of merit."

The third point, the way to perform a gathering offering, consists of a condensed presentation and an elaborate explanation. Concerning the former, a *gathering* of fortunate individuals collects a *gathering* of precious materials and offers this to the *gathering* of deities that are being accomplished, thereby perfecting the *gatherings* of merit and wisdom.

The longer explanation divides this offering into preliminary activities, the main practice, and concluding activities. For the preliminary activities, arrange a vast maṇḍala in a suitable place to perform the profound activities of mantra. This can also consist of the supports of exalted body, speech, and mind, or piles of flowers equal to the number of deities. Having blessed the maṇḍala, gather suitable substances for the outer, inner, and secret offerings, whatever materials for the gathering one can afford. At the very least there should be meat and alcohol, as these two are indispensable. Representing method and wisdom, male and female practitioners who possess samayas should then gather in equal numbers. There should be at least two practitioners, but it is better to have many. Regardless of how many there are, the male and female practitioners must be equal in number, otherwise it is not a genuine feast offering. If there are mostly heroes present, it is merely called a "celebration of heroes," and when the participants are mostly heroines, it is termed a "banquet of heroines."

Next, practitioners who are worthy to assemble should wear the dress of the peaceful or wrathful deity on which their flower fell. As they enter the hall for the feast, there should be people placed at the four gates, dressed like wrathful deities, who will ask them if they are welcome in a symbolic manner by raising one finger. To reply that they are welcome, the practitioners raise two fingers and then enter.

Once inside, the activity vajra will ask them what buddha family they belong to by showing the gesture of the three-pronged vajra. In response, practitioners will show the gesture of the main deity of the buddha family on which their flower fell. The practitioners then make prostrations to the vajra master and take their seats in rows based on when empowerment was received, their mastery of wisdom, and other such factors. The rows are situated to the left, right, and in front of the leader. Symbolic implements and other items are placed at the rows, illustrating the five families. Once the practitioners have been seated in the row of their respective buddha family, the activity vajra prostrates and supplications are made to remain in the maṇḍala of meditative stabilization. These are the preliminary activities.

The main part of the gathering begins by offering the torma to the obstructing forces and closing the boundaries, as spelled out in detail in the ritual manual. Offerings for the feast are cleansed, purified, multiplied, transformed, and offered to the deities, which are indivisible from oneself. Then the activity vajra makes prostrations and distributes the substances of means and knowledge using the lotus gesture. The play of receiving these symbols with symbols satiates all deities of the aggregates, elements, and sense bases with undefiled great bliss.

During the feast offering, one should abandon fixation on ordinary appearances and rest continuously in the play of deity, mantra, and meditative absorption. One must also refrain from any kind of prank, chatter, and mockery, and enjoy the feast substances within equality free from any concepts of pure and impure. Vajra songs, vajra dances, the union of empty bliss, and other offerings may be made at this point in accord with one's meditation experience. In short, the feast encompasses the entire range of outer, inner, secret, and suchness offerings.

For the concluding activities, all leftovers from the feast are carried out and offered as a torma. Finally, the vajra songs, dances, and other concluding activities of the maṇḍala should be performed in their entirety.

3. Principle

The unsurpassed offerings of secret mantra are more exalted than the offerings made in the lower vehicles because they are superior with regard to the object to whom they are directed, the intention, and the things that are offered. The object that these offerings are given to is the ultimate field of merit—buddhahood itself. If one knows that all phenomena within appearance and existence are the spontaneously present great maṇḍala of primordial purity, then the entirety of existence and peace is satiated in equality, even if one makes offerings to just one deity. Likewise, enjoying an object while one's body, speech, and mind are in the form of the three vajras is identical to making offerings to the Buddha as such. For this reason, it is superior. Moreover, buddhas have a body of the wisdom of equality and do not entertain any concepts of being pleased or displeased. Nevertheless, in accordance with the inclinations and interests of those in need of guidance, they assume a perfect wisdom body. Therefore, by greatly pleasing the deities of mantra, the two spiritual attainments are easily attained.

In terms of intention, enjoyment without fixated grasping takes place within the state of the great purity and equality of suchness. Thereby, generosity and the rest of the perfections, as well as faith, compassion, and all the other elements that cause great awakening, without exception become the embodiment of the single taste of great bliss and emptiness endowed with all supreme aspects.

Since all phenomena are enjoyed without any form of clinging or restraint, this constitutes the effortless spontaneous accomplishment of the perfection of *generosity* as well as its fruition. In the same way, realizing equality allows one to remain unsurpassed and untainted by any fault. Hence, this involves *discipline* as well. It also encompasses *patience*, insofar as one is undisturbed and the signs of wisdom are complete. It is *diligence* in that there is no decay and the activities become the accumulations. *Meditative concentration* is included because one does not stray from the state of equality, even though one's faculties engage with objects, and since one dwells in the observation of the nature of all phenomena. It is also *knowledge* because the nature is realized just as it is, whereby all phenomena are known without any obstruction and one is beyond conceptualizing objects. *Method* is present insofar as the benefit of self and others is effortlessly performed. *Aspiration* is included since realms and experiences are utterly pure. *Strength* is present since it can never be subdued by any opposing factors. Finally, it is *wisdom* because one genuinely realizes the nature, whereby all dualistic phenomena disappear into nonduality.

Moreover, the approach of remaining nondual with buddhahood itself, in which one spontaneously accomplishes activity for the benefit and happiness of all beings in all times and places, allows for the spontaneous presence of faith, compassion, and all the other qualities of the path. In this way, the intention of this form of offering is superior as well.

As for the things that are offered, since all offering substances are transformed into the nectar of wisdom, they are no longer ordinary. As natural purity and equality, they can appear in any possible form out of reality, which is nothing whatsoever. For this reason, offerings can be transformed through visualization, mantras, and gestures, such that one can present Samantabhadra's cloudbank of offerings in the space of just a single atom, offering infinite riches found in the buddha fields that fill the reaches of space, an inexhaustible treasure of great bliss.

4. Purpose

This unique method of truly delighting the deities of secret mantra enables one to effortlessly gain all the spiritual attainments of action and wisdom. Offerings are extremely important because they are the gateway to fully perfecting the accumulations of merit and wisdom. In short, offering is what pleases the wisdom deities, while the ultimate method for pleasing them is to access the nature of mantra. The *Sūtra That Gathers All Intents* says:

> To internalize merely one
> Of the secret words of the great vehicle
> Far surpasses sending vast offerings,
> Even if greatly multiplied,
> To an inconceivable number of beings and listeners,
> And limitless buddhas and bodhisattvas.
> Why? Because knowing the great vehicle
> Is the best way to please the victorious ones.

Therefore, there is no other path of mantra that is not an offering of practice, wealth, or service. As such, the categories renowned as the eleven parameters of training can be included in the offerings explained in this context: the three parameters of the path—view, absorption, and conduct; the three parameters that maintain the foundation—maṇḍala, empowerment, and samaya; the three practices—accomplishment, offering, and enlightened activity; and the two methods—mantra and mudrā. Since the other ten topics are truly suitable to be condensed within offering, offering encompasses them all. Still, in terms of its distinct essential nature, it can also be explained as an individual topic, separate from the other trainings.

In the nature of reality—great purity and equality—there is no fixation on something that is offered, one who offers, and the act of offering. The perfection of all offerings should be understood to take place within the nature of the great perfection—the expansive, self-manifesting array of the self-display, within the great, natural spontaneous presence. In the nature of the great perfection, this is known as the perfection of all offerings. The *Tantra of the Secret Essence* states:

> Stability in the magical net
> Delights the entire range of maṇḍalas
> Of the buddhas of the ten directions and four times,
> And manifests for the beings of the three realms.

This concludes the teaching on the topic of offering, the perfection of generosity.

9. Enlightened Activity

This ninth section discusses enlightened activity in terms of its (1) essence, (2) divisions, (3) principle, and (4) purpose.

1. Essence

Concerning the first of these, the *Tantra of the Secret Essence* states:

> Since knowledge, the suchness of the expanse,
> Becomes the mudrā of method,
> Wisdom plays within wisdom,
> Yet this very play of wisdom is unreal.
> The manifest appearance and protection of victorious ones,
> As well as the show of blessings are just so.
> With the splendor capable of action,
> There is illusion, supreme vajra majesty.

The Sanskrit word *karma* means physical, verbal, and mental actions. This refers to the extraordinary activities of skillful methods that focus primarily on working for the welfare of others. Such activity is imbued with the relative awakened mind, which is elicited by the four immeasurables and great knowledge.

2. Divisions

In terms of its goal, enlightened activity can be either supreme or common. Supreme enlightened activity involves planting the seed of liberation in another's being by initiating him or her into a maṇḍala, using mantras and mudrās, or by other such means. Common enlightened activities include everything that brings about a pleasant, albeit temporary, result.

When divided in terms of support, enlightened activities may utilize either external substances or the internal body, speech, and mind. There are innumerable activities that utilize various external substances. Such substances include drawings of magical circles, fire offerings, stūpas, statues, symbolic implements, corpses, and the five meats. Activities may also be accomplished using physical mudrās, dances, expressions, gazes, postures, and other such actions; by verbally reciting mantras, singing, uttering words of truth, and so on; and mentally through intention and absorption. Moreover, enlightened activities may be carried out by utilizing each of these individually or by using them all in conjunction with one another. By carrying out the activities of mantra in harmony with the mind-sets of sentient beings, one will be able to accomplish both temporal and ultimate aims. Hence, when classified further in terms of internal divisions and the aims of the activity, the varieties of enlightened activity are limitless.

In terms of essence, there are four types of enlightened activity that either benefit or annihilate: pacifying, enriching, magnetizing, and subjugating. Pacifying activities include pacifying illness, malevolent forces, negativity, obscurations, enemies, fears, obstacles, black magic, and so forth. Enriching activities are designed to cause lifespan, merit, wisdom, splendor, retinue, wealth, strength, prosperity, happiness, dharma, and other such factors to flourish. Magnetizing activities are used to bring something or someone under one's control. This may include humans, such as kings, ministers, queens, or scholars; nonhuman beings, including gods, serpent beings, and malevolent spirits; glory, such as experience, realization, and enlightened qualities; and material goods like food, drink, clothing, and jewelry. There are various forms of subjugating activity as well. These include summoning, separating, binding, suppressing, averting, killing, and expelling; terrorizing, such as destroying something or driving someone insane; and creating bad omens, lightning, hail, and so on.

In terms of qualities, any act may be ordinary or supreme. The former refers to acts motivated by the three poisons, such as attachment to one's own welfare. In essence, such acts are not embraced with the purposeful activity of skillful methods, nor do they lead to a meaningful result, either temporarily or ultimately. Though they may look like mantric activities on the surface, in truth they are ordinary acts. In this context, such acts are to be avoided.

Supreme activities, in contrast, are directed toward the welfare of others and are motivated by great compassion. In essence, they are characterized by the intent and conduct of mantra, which are embraced by extraordinary methods and knowledge. The results of such acts are deeply meaningful on both a temporal and ultimate level and are accomplished with ease.

Those knowledge holders who swiftly accomplish buddhahood for the welfare of all sentient beings may liberate the enemies and obstructive forces that create obstacles on their path. They may also accomplish activities that pacify their own illnesses and so forth, thereby directly benefiting themselves and indirectly benefiting others. Because they are embraced by profound intent and conduct, such acts are not inferior in terms of their cause, essence, or fruition.

On the other hand, this is not the case with other acts, such as reversing mantras directed at the personal enemies of the three jewels. Though such acts may seem to benefit others in a temporary sense, in terms of their cause, essence, and fruition they are in line with ordinary acts. Hence, they should be avoided.

Therefore, knowledge involves knowing the right time to initiate an act, such that it does not conflict with the path; knowing how to carry out the act; and being skilled when it comes to transforming the result of the activity into the path of enlightenment. Method, on the other hand, is the supreme strength needed to carry out the activity, which may be mantra, mudrā, or otherwise, as well as embracing the act with the profound viewpoint and conduct of mantra. In this way, when embraced by both means and knowledge, accomplishing a given act with ease is the temporal result, while the gradual accomplishment of enlightenment is its ultimate fruition.

The activities of the buddhas also benefit and create happiness for sentient beings, both temporally and ultimately. Engaging in buddha activity means to not let such acts become something to hope for in the future, but instead to carry out such activities here and now by utilizing the skillful methods of mantra. Ordinary bodhisattvas, for example, are unable to directly benefit those who have amassed extremely negative karma or savages who have gone completely astray. Aside from merely making aspiration prayers to benefit them in the future, they will be powerless to help them. Here, however, the skillful method of wrathful liberation can be used to directly cut through the stream of negative karma. Similarly, one is able to use the methods of mantra to manifest pacifying and other forms of activity as well, and to do so just as one intends and aspires. This is the enlightened activity of secret mantra. The *Tantra of the Secret Essence* states:

> This itself is the self-display of wisdom:
> Names, words, forms and the like, just as one intends,
> Like light appearing in darkness,
> Alchemical transformation and medicine.

Furthermore, the aspiration prayers made by bodhisattvas are infinite because they need to bring about the temporal and ultimate well-being of all sentient beings, doing so in harmony with the variations in character, aptitude, and aspiration that beings possess. In a similar manner, the enlightened activities of secret mantra are also infinite. By utilizing mantras, specific aspiration prayers can be brought to fruition. For this reason, this is also the perfection of aspiration. The same point is made in the *Ornament of the Mahāyāna Sūtras*:

> The aspiration prayers of the steadfast
> Are intention along with aspiration.

And:

> As soon as it comes from the mind, it has an effect.

3. Principle

This topic is divided into (1) the superior approach, (2) the middling approach, and (3) the ordinary approach. The superior approach is accomplished by utilizing the completion stage. Those with knowledge who are of the very highest capacity are capable of accessing the nature of the great perfection without signs. These practitioners of the path of liberation are able to gain mastery over all phenomena of saṃsāra and nirvāṇa. This takes place once they obtain the empowerment into the display of self-awareness, thereby resolving all phenomena within the expanse of the innate nature of one's own mind. With this ability, they need not work or strain to achieve their desired aims. Instead, they accomplish their aims by merely wishing to do so. Even if they have yet to attain this degree of mastery, their acts will become supreme by imbuing all actions with this view.

By familiarizing themselves with the completion stage with signs, diligent individuals may gain the form of the energetic mind by merging two factors: the energies (referred to as "life force") and form (meaning empty forms). Once this has come to pass, what they focus on will actually appear once they merely direct their attention to a remedial deity or another such factor. Through this, they will be able to accomplish the activity they are engaged in with ease, whatever its purpose may be.

In the middling approach, activities are accomplished utilizing the development stage. Once the coarse and subtle clear appearances of the development stage alone have reached a point of perfection, one will be able to use supportive factors like mantras and mudrās to attain the entire range of worldly spiritual attainments, all the way up to those of the Unexcelled Realms. If the development stage is accomplished in this manner, one can carry out various activities simply through visualization.

In the ordinary approach, activities are accomplished through mantra recitation. Here, individuals who have received empowerment and not let their samayas degenerate use a ritual and recite secret mantras through the medium of faith. When performed in this manner, one will be able to accomplish various activities through the power of mantra, just as one wishes. Concerning the use of ritual, if we use an activity that pacifies illness to illustrate this process, various factors, such as precise substances and visualizations, are employed in the recitation of mantra. These details are clearly mentioned in each individual tantra. Without such rituals, moreover, activities will not be accomplished because the requisite causes and conditions will not be complete. Even if they are accomplished, their effects will be greatly delayed. On this approach, the *Root Tantra of Mañjuśrī* explains:

> Whether the state of a divine master,
> Or that of a master who is never divine,

> Such states can be accomplished through mantras.
> Still, if the ritual is skipped, their potency is lost.

And:

> Through mantra endowed with ritual,
> Accomplishments are swiftly and fully obtained.

And:

> It is held that by practicing mantra without ritual,
> Once, after spinning in circles for long,
> At some point accomplishment will be gained.

Furthermore, it goes without saying that mantra will be accomplished if one is able to visualize in a precise manner. Yet even if one's visualization is nothing more than merely devoted training, mantra will still be accomplished if one has faith. Without faith, on the other hand, accomplishment is impossible. The previous text states:

> Without faith in mantra,
> Though one may exert oneself in various ways,
> Mantras will not be accomplished.
> Thus, samaya is not to be taught to the wicked.

Furthermore, as far as faith goes, it should go without saying what will happen if one has faith free of doubt concerning the profound points, such as the conviction of knowing deity and mantra to be inseparable. On this point, the *Tantra of the Three Practices of Yama's Black Enemy* states:

> Spiritual attainment is near for those with expertise
> That is free from doubt concerning the nature
> Of the inconceivable reality.

Even if one lacks this understanding, accomplishment is also possible if one faithfully recites one-pointedly and without hesitation, thinking to oneself: "This is how it is in the scriptures." The same text states:

> Alternatively, an ignoramus with stable faith
> Is near to the spiritual attainment of joining.

On the other hand, spiritual attainment will not manifest for those who have lost faith. Such individuals lack the knowledge that comes from seeing the profound nature of mantra in an accurate manner. Harboring a stubborn tendency to scrutinize in a way that obstructs spiritual attainment, they question mantra and its rituals, analyzing them in various ways. The text then reads:

> Intellectuals who ponder and analyze
> Are far from the spiritual attainment of application.
> Though the guru may teach key instructions,
> If a student falls prey to indecision,
> It is taught that spiritual attainments are far away.
> Though the guru may conceal key instructions,
> If a student is not consumed by indecision
> And regards the guru's key instructions as sacred,
> Holding them in great esteem, attainment is certain.

And:

> If one analyzes the application of mantras and substances,
> Spiritual attainments will not occur.
> If one is consumed by indecision,
> Has a fickle mind, or waning faith,
> Even if attainment is close at that time,
> One will undoubtedly revert back.

Therefore, faith is extremely important when it comes to mantra recitation. If one recites with faith, there will be accomplishment in mantra. If mantra is accomplished, one will attain the body of a knowledge holder of the desire or form realm and become immortal. In terms of speech, one will attain words of truth. Realization, moreover, will arise in the mind, and gradually one's fortune will be equal to that of the superior deity. Hence, one must be diligent in faithfully reciting mantras. The same text explains:

> If one practices with stable faith,
> Even if space itself disappears,
> The absence of the spiritual attainments of mantra is not possible.
> Since it is not possible to be deceived by the awareness mantras
> Taught by the deities and sages,
> Deceit by the application of the secret mantras
> Taught by those devoid of attachment
> Has not happened, nor will it.

And:

> Faith is the Buddha, faith is dharma,
> Faith is saṅgha, and faith is mother;
> Faith is the guru, faith is the father,
> Faith is the highway, faith is a ship,
> And faith is a wish-fulfilling jewel.
> Faith is the spiritual attainment of secret mantra.
> Faith is the wealth of merit itself.
> Therefore, the practitioner of mantra,
> In order to arouse faith in the mind,
> Should honor others with respect.

The better the causes and conditions of the mantra ritual are, such as having a stable visualization and so forth, the swifter and more powerful the accomplishment of mantra will be. However, one should know that even a mantra recited out of mere faith, which is the minimum, enacts various activities. There are, moreover, various activities that are accomplished by means of substances alone, such as magnetizing someone or something. When these are embraced by the profound viewpoint and conduct of secret mantra, they may become mere subsidiary parts of an activity. Nevertheless, they are not the genuine activities that utilize the skillful methods of mantra, as is the case with the medicines explained in the art of healing.

4. Purpose

Based on the skillful methods of mantra, all desired objectives become accomplished in accord with one's wishes. In this way the path is quickly and easily perfected. Hence, such enlightened activity has the exalted power, wondrous qualities, and function of the path of mantra. As written in the *Accomplishment of the Single Hero Mañjuśrī*:

> The practitioner of mantra, like a wish-fulfilling jewel,
> Works diligently and benefits sentient beings.

To summarize, the basis for such wondrous enlightened activity comes from having been empowered into a maṇḍala and having abided by one's samayas. Enlightened activity must be accomplished by embracing whatever sādhana one is using with the view, meditation, and conduct, and not being without accomplishment, offering, mantra, and mudrā. Therefore, since all paths are subsumed under the basis of enlightened activity and its system of methods, enlightened activity does not dispense with any of these but encompasses them all. Ultimately, when one dwells effortlessly in the basic space of the great perfection of natural equality, without focusing on an action, agent, or object, enlightened activity will be effortless and spontaneously perfected. The *Tantra of the Secret Essence* states:

> The imputations of mistaken ideas are completely pure,
> And wisdom is none other than basic space.
> Thus, a link is formed through great compassion
> That appears to the six classes in every time and place.

This concludes the explanation of the topic of enlightened activity, the perfection of aspiration prayers.

10. Mudrā
This tenth section discusses mudrā in terms of its (1) essence, (2) divisions, (3) principle, and (4) function.

1. Essence
Concerning the first of these, the *Tantra of the Secret Essence* states:

> Completely perfect through the magical net,
> Everything is sealed with supreme enlightenment.

>   As the secret reality ascertained,
>   The seal of the essence is difficult to transgress.

The word "seal" derives from the Sanskrit term *mudrā*, which means either to implant and symbolize, or a seal that is difficult to transgress. This refers to the extraordinary means that symbolize the enlightened body, speech, mind, and activities of great beings. When something is implanted with such a symbol, it becomes an embodiment of it and is difficult to transgress.

2. Divisions
This section has three parts: (1) a general presentation, (2) a specific presentation, and (3) a special presentation.

1. General Presentation
The general presentation concerns the seals of the (1) ground, (2) path, and (3) fruition. As for the seals of the ground, the natural seal of reality is the primordial purity of the nature of mind. Within the state of the great seal, sights, sounds, and awareness dwell as the nature of the deity, mantra, and dharma body.

The temporary seal of the path is used to refine one's experience of this nature. To this end, one establishes body, speech, and mind to be the play of the three secrets. This is done within the state of vajra wisdom, the reality of mind, the great seal of co-emergent great bliss.

The ultimate seal of the fruition occurs when one has discovered all aspects of the body of self-occurring wisdom. At this point one acts with the inconceivable enlightened body, speech, mind, and activities for the welfare of all infinite sentient beings that fill the entirety of space.

2. Specific Presentation
When discussed in detail, the seals of the path can be linked with either the development stage or the completion stage.

1. Seals in the Development Stage
In the development stage, there is the great seal of enlightened form, the dharma seal of enlightened speech, the samaya seal of enlightened mind, and the action seal of enlightened activity.

2. Seals in the Completion Stage

This is explained in terms of (1) the support of a spiritual consort, (2) the path where the seals manifest, and (3) the fruition of the four wisdoms. First is the support of the spiritual consort. Here the dharma seal is emptiness, the nature of all phenomena. This feminine perfection of knowledge is the true spiritual partner. The action seal refers to everyone that appears in female form with long hair, breasts, and so forth. The samaya seal is the mudrā of wisdom, the goddess emanated from one's own mind. The great seal is the empty form of the energetic mind, the nature of which manifests as the goddess. Sealing with these mudrās brings about the attainment of unchanging bliss.

Second is the path where the seals manifest. Here the action seal serves as the support for the attainment of great bliss, symbolic wisdom. This includes union with a spiritual consort. Through such acts one comes to experience a mere approximation of the great bliss of the basic space of phenomena. This experience is the dharma seal. The great seal is to be free of all conceptual thought and to directly experience the innate. That which appears out of this state as the maṇḍala of enlightened body, speech, and mind in the ensuing attainment is the samaya seal.

This can also be applied to the four joys: joy, supreme joy, innate joy, and joyless joy. In the tantras, joyless joy is presented as the third stage. Nevertheless, here this refers to the state of joylessness that occurs once the pangs of desire have been exhausted. One may then wonder whether or not this contradicts the four joys as presented in all other scriptures. There is, however, no contradiction. Both systems hold that *innate* refers to an instant of wisdom that transcends any dichotomies of desire and nondesire, bliss and nonbliss. This occurs in the interval between the complete and total culmination of joy, which is brought about by bodhicitta descending to the tip of the jewel vajra, and the initial onset of desirelessness. Therefore, there is no contradiction in presenting the first three joys as four divisions, nor is there any contradiction in condensing the four joys into three instances. These correlations are discussed in Nāgārjuna's *Ascertaining the Four Seals*.

Third is the fruition of the four wisdoms. Here the vajra body of appearance and emptiness is the action seal. The vajra speech of clarity and emptiness is the dharma seal. The vajra mind of bliss and emptiness is the samaya seal. The vajra wisdom of awareness and emptiness—the essential indivisible equality of all of these—is the great seal.

Hence, there are numerous ways to correlate the four seals in terms of significance and context. There are also innumerable names used to express different seals, such as "the seal with signs" and "the seal without signs."

3. Special Presentation
In this context, it is primarily specific hand gestures that are being taught. Such hand mudrās serve to represent all the various forms of enlightened body, speech, mind, and activities of the wisdom deity. Since this also carries the meaning of nontransgression, here a general term is applied to a specific instance. The subclassifications of this division also encompass the four seals. The essence of the mudrā that is being shown is the samaya seal. Acts, such as transforming and releasing, are the action seal. Visualizing such things as the seed and reciting mantra is the dharma seal. Finally, one's own presence as the form of the deity is the great seal.

The foundation of all mudrās that are held by joining the two palms together is to either join one's palms or to perform the vajra gesture, which is made by interlacing the fingers and joining the palms. The foundation of all mudrās that are held with the hands apart is the vajra fist, in which the thumbs are placed inside and with the other fingers wrapped around them. Various root and subsidiary mudrās derive from these. Root mudrās include those of peaceful deities, such as those of the five buddha families, as well as those of wrathful deities. The various subsidiary mudrās include those of invitation, bestowal of empowerment, and making offerings. In a beautiful and elegant manner, such mudrās should be integrated with the revolving lotus, the dancing lotus, and other such mudrās. Once completed, they should be released with a snap of the fingers.

3. Principle
This section explains (1) the principle of the seals and (2) how they are used to seal.

1. Understanding the Principle of the Seals
Seals can be classified in six ways according to scripture and the viewpoints of specific individuals. The first position holds that mantras and mudrās are differentiated in terms of their relation to ripened body or speech. In other words, a physical feature is termed mudrā, whereas a verbal expression is termed mantra. Hence, they state that such physical and verbal expressions are merely perceptible instances of the ordinary body and speech.

The second position holds that these are symbols that represent the enlightened body, speech, and mind of the victorious ones, just as meaning can be conveyed through a gesture of the hand or a name.

The third holds that such symbols possess the ability to bring about the spiritual attainments of activity and wisdom. Hence, they are thought of as mere instances of infallible interdependent origination.

In the fourth position, mudrās and mantras are considered to be expressions of one's own karma and, thus, included within ordinary body and speech. Nevertheless, such expressions are also recognized to manifest from the strength of the blessings of the thus-gone ones. Take, for example, the evil demon that was blessed by Mañjuśrī and subsequently gave teachings on the great vehicle. The sounds of his words were part of his own being, yet they also manifested from the blessings of the Noble One. Just so, those who hold this position consider mudrās and mantras to manifest from the blessings of the thus-gone ones, while being mixed with one's own karmic perceptions.

In the fifth position, mudrā and mantra are likened to the moon's reflection. When the moon's reflection appears in a bucket of water, its image may seem to be in the water. Nevertheless, it is nothing more than the moon's manifestation. Similarly, mantras and mudrās manifest from the blessings of the thus-gone ones and have the potential to bring about spiritual attainments. When those with samaya imagine themselves to be the deity itself and practice accordingly, a connection with the actual deity occurs in correspondence with their grasping. In this sense, mudrās and mantras function without fail, in the same way that an actual object can be brought about through grasping at an object universal. In a similar manner, those who hold this position think that the deity itself can be accomplished from these symbols.

The sixth position holds that mantras and mudrās are the manifestation of the ultimate form of the victorious ones, the great wisdom of totality. Wisdom appears in this way having been blessed by the power of compassion and aspiration, just as the mind itself may manifest as objects and forms due to habitual tendencies. Hence, those who hold this position consider mantra and mudrā to be divine in essence. In other words, they hold that there is no actual difference between mantra and mudrā and a deity that has attained the form of wisdom.

Each of these six is superior to the previous position. Those who hold the sixth position, which is supreme to all the rest, accurately understand the principles of mantra and mudrā. Hence, the principles of mantra and mudrā should be understood in this way alone.

2. Understanding How Mudrās Are Used to Seal

This section discusses (1) the reason for sealing and (2) the way to seal. First, as for the reason for sealing, in outer mantra, mudrās have three aspects. In terms of *cause*, they are emanated images of the utterly pure basic space of phenomena and great wisdom. In *essence*, they represent the infinite gateways to complete liberation. In terms of *result*, they have the potential to bring about all activities and spiritual attainments. Hence, mudrās are the signs of great beings. They cannot be transgressed or destroyed by anyone or anything. They are the extraordinary seal of the sovereign king of dharma and are able to accomplish all forms of buddha activity.

Therefore, when one's being is sealed with a mudrā, it will be freed from its bonds. The city of ignorance, the great negative force, will be conquered. The body will be stable and negative forces will be completely unable to affect it. Empowerments that are bestowed will be attained and activities will be accomplished without going to waste. If one does not lose sight of their nature, the samayas will not degenerate. Furthermore, since mudrās also possess the symbol of the feminine, they are the hidden form of female deities. If they are shown to someone, they will be delighted by the very essence of samaya. Mudrās are used to seal for these and other reasons.

Mudrās also fulfill these same purposes in inner mantra as well. Nevertheless, according to this system they are primarily used to seal for the following reasons: Within the state of great wisdom—the spontaneously present mudrā—emanated mudrās are applied to rouse the awakened mind of great bliss, the indivisible nature of all bliss-gone ones and sentient beings, which dwells in the hearts of all beings. They also bring about the effortless attainment of extraordinary mastery and carry out various enlightened buddha activities for the benefit of other beings just as one desires.

Secondly, as for the way to seal, according to outer mantra, when the reality of one's being is sealed with a mudrā that symbolizes the deity, one will actually become the deity through the power of blessings. This is likened to the seal of a royal decree, which cannot be transgressed once enacted.

In inner mantra, the mudrā is essentially the deity. As the mudrā seals the indivisibility of oneself and the deity, deity dissolves into deity; reality merges with reality; and wisdom revels in wisdom. Through this, one becomes the deity and the deity, in essence, becomes oneself. In this manner, methods are used to awaken and actualize the great bliss that dwells within.

4. Purpose

Utilizing these unique methods allows one to accomplish all temporal and ultimate aims and carry out the activity of the buddhas. For this reason, they possess supreme qualities. In brief, by virtue of what they represent, mudrās subsume all dharmas of the ground, path, and fruition. This unique method of mantra is to be maintained by receiving the bestowed empowerment into a maṇḍala and abiding by the samayas. As such, it should be kept completely concealed from others. Mudrā accords with the view and meditation and is a particular instance of conduct and accomplishment. Mudrā is also the single unsurpassed method for pleasing the deity, carrying out activities, and arousing the power of mantra. Hence, it relates to all paths.

In the ultimate meaning, all phenomena and all movements of body, speech, and mind are perfect and do not have to be transformed, bound, or released. As such, they are effortlessly perfected as the nature of mudrā. As stated in the *Tantra of the Secret Essence*:

> When the supreme gathering of the great seal
> Is joined with the endowment of means and knowledge,
> Motionless and unmoving, everything
> Dwells in the state of the great seal.

And in the *Awesome Flash of Lightning*:

> When dwelling in a state of equality with the intrinsic nature,
> All movements and motions
> Are mudrā, so the hero has said.

This concludes the section on the great method of mudrā.

11. Mantra

This section has four parts: (1) essence, (2) divisions, (3) accessing the principle of mantra, and (4) purpose.

1. Essence
Concerning the essence of mantra, the *Tantra of the Secret Essence* states:

> A itself appears in manifold forms,
> As KA and the rest of the forty-two letters.
> The names of these sounds are all-inclusive
> And are themselves surely the perfect complete king.

The Sanskrit term *mantra* means, "to protect consciousness" or "protect the mind." Thus, mantras link the knowledge of consciousness with the method of protecting. Alternatively, mantras can be said to protect the mental consciousness efficiently and swiftly. In short, the term *mantra* refers to an extraordinary method.

Here, in the context of discussing the essence of mantra, it refers to the essence of the mantra that is repeated using the letters of method and knowledge. Since this essence is established in four ways, it has the unimpeded ability to accomplish spiritual attainments. To briefly elaborate, mantras (1) are caused by letters, (2) are essentially established in four ways, and (3) have unimpeded ability in terms of effect.

1. Letters: The Cause of Mantras
First, in essence, the nature of distinct sound units are A and the rest of the sixteen vowels of knowledge, and the thirty-four consonants of method, such as the letter KA. These fifty letters are the basis and source of all letters. Since OṂ and other such syllables are formations of these letters and are themselves letters by nature, they as well can be referred to as such.

Secondly, letters can be divided into four categories: letters that are present in the channels of the body, letters of the palace and deities, letters of magical emanation, and letters of symbolic words. The first refers to the way in which letters are present in the radial channels of the body, as stated in the tantras. In this particular tantra, the syllables OṂ, ĀḤ, and HŪṂ are said to be located at the three places. Letters of the palace and deities are the seed syllables that one visualizes at certain places in the maṇḍala when meditating on a deity. Letters of magical emanation are clouds of letters that radiate out from the three secrets of the enjoyment body buddhas; they act for the welfare of beings through manifold emanations. Letters of symbolic words are the verbal expressions of the individual sounds of a mantra. This also includes the verbal expressions based on the sounds of the words that are present within the ground, as well as the forms that symbolize them that are used in meditation. In the state of complete purity, clouds of letters manifest as the self-display of the wisdom of fruition.

2. The Four Establishments: The Essence of Mantra

Second is the explanation of the essence of mantra. Generally, the various conventional meanings subsumed within the states of thorough affliction and complete purification can be elucidated using combinations of letters. Hence, all buddha activities are either directly or indirectly accomplished using such letters. For this reason, among the objects experienced by worldly individuals, there is nothing more powerful or wondrous than letters. Relatively, these expressive and elucidating interdependent appearances are unceasing. Ultimately, however, there is nothing to express and thus no expressions either. Since these expressions themselves are not established in the slightest, they do not express anything at all. Even if this equality of the two truths is seen in terms of a single syllable, through this the four gateways of retention will be attained.

More specifically, the mantras uttered by the Buddha are established in four ways: they are established by (1) the essence of reality itself, (2) by the nature of the subject, (3) through blessings, and (4) through power and force. The first refers to the primordial essence of all letters being the equality of great emptiness. The second refers to the essence of each letter having an incontrovertible nature that manifests in a unique manner. These first two do not apply solely to mantras, but to all phenomena. Nevertheless, by virtue of these two facts, mantras are capable of affording blessings and unimpeded power. This, in turn, is due to the incontrovertible principles of interdependence and reality itself. The latter, while being nothing at all, can give rise to the former, which can manifest as anything. The third refers to the fact that letters are established by the blessings of the buddhas. In attaining mastery over all phenomena, the buddhas emanate their own wisdom in the form of mantras, which vary in length from one letter up to many. Finally, the fourth refers to the fact that mantras, just like the power of medicines and jewels, possess the incontrovertible and unimpeded power to bring about the achievement of spiritual attainments.

Since all verbalizations are primordially present in a state of purity and equality, in terms of the natural state, all manifestations of language are the maṇḍala of enlightened speech. To this, one may object that all the verbal expressions of sentient beings should have these same beneficial effects. Sentient beings, however, do not realize this. Thus, not only do these beneficial effects not occur, their verbal expressions actually become a cause for their own bondage as they fixate on these self-displays as being ordinary. This is similar to the way fear might arise if one takes a rope to be a snake. This same principle holds for the relationships between movements and mudrā; between food, drink, and feast offerings; and so forth.

One may also wonder whether or not the mantras created by the buddhas and those created by Brahma and other such figures are equal in strength. There is a difference between these two categories from the point of view of appearance, as the former are blessed by the buddhas to benefit those in need of guidance. Those mantras that are determined to be such by valid scriptures are unparalleled.

One may further object that since all sounds are symbolic gateways to complete liberation, the number of mantras taught with respect to those in need of guidance should also be limitless. Moreover, since the root letters are blessed, all that is derived from such syllables would be said to be mantra. Yet again, since the Buddha's enlightened speech, in all its various forms, knows no partiality or bias, everything would be enlightened speech. If this is the case, the objection goes, why should mantra recitation have different effects than ordinary chatter and so forth?

Mantras, however, are believed to be divine and are recited with faith for this reason, whereas this is not the case with other forms of speech. Moreover, if a mantra is thought to be something ordinary and not seen for what it is, it will not be able to perform its intended function. Mantras are like nonconceptual wish-fulfilling jewels. Infusing one's being with the blessings of mantra, like the form of a moon reflected on a body of water, necessitates the presence of faith and other conditions that set the stage for the spiritual attainments of mantra. Just as the moon's reflection cannot appear without water, mantras cannot function without the presence of faith and other such factors in one's being.

Nevertheless, this is not to say that simply hearing the sound of the Thus-Gone One's awareness mantras through the power of the inconceivable emanations of the Buddha is completely pointless. The *Fundamental Intent of Mañjuśrī* explains:

Reciting the mantras of the thus-gone ones
Is, in this way, beneficial.
Even those who throw a glance,
Will become followers.

Therefore, from the perspective of the way things appear conventionally, blessings occur once the mantras of the Buddha's teachings come together with one's own devoted interest. Because the right causes and conditions have been assembled, blessings do indeed arise, just as a sprout will shoot up once a seed, water, and the other necessary conditions are in place, and like the blessings that occur when an individual with a pure being meets with a disciple who sees him or her as realized.

3. Unimpeded Ability: The Effect of Mantra
It is not the case that the mantras established in this way do not have the power to accomplish both temporal and ultimate goals, the reason being that mantras are the essence of the deity. Therefore, even at the level of an ordinary being, that which invokes the supportive strength of the thus-gone ones and carries out various activities is mantra. For those with ordinary experiential domains, when it comes to bringing about spiritual attainment, there is nothing in the world equal to mantra. Brahma, Īśvara, wish-fulfilling trees, jewels, and other such things … none of these can compete with even a fraction of mantra's power. The profound view, meditation, and other such factors are objects only of those who have pure beings; they are not within the reach of common beings. Mantras, however, can be recited by all.

This concludes the explanation of the essence of mantras.

2. Divisions
This section has three parts: (1) general divisions, (2) specific divisions, and (3) special divisions.

1. General Divisions
The general division concerns the ground, path, and fruition. As for the ground, all phenomena dwell primordially as great purity and equality, complete within the state of great bliss of the nature of one's very own mind. This naturally luminous maṇḍala of the mind is termed "the reality of mantra." This is the mantra of the ground. The path of mantra refers to all paths

in which mantras are used to swiftly and efficiently protect the mind by utilizing the extraordinary practices of method and knowledge to actualize the mantra of the ground. The fruition is the actualization of the nature of mind as great bliss, the enlightened body of great wisdom. In being a sacred refuge and protector for all beings, it provides them all with benefit and happiness.

2. Specific Divisions
The term *mantra* can refer to various objects. The nature free from constructs, for example, may be called *mantra*. In the *Complete Enlightenment of Vairocana*, to give another example, the nature free from constructs is referred to as the very identity of secret mantra. Nondual wisdom is also termed *mantra*. The same tantra states:

> This very nondual wisdom
> The Sage referred to as *mantra*.

Also, the bodies of the deities that symbolize this nature are likewise referred to as *mantra*. The same text explains:

> To all these very mantras as well,
> Offer wondrous tormas.

Furthermore, collections of scripture, as well as burnt offerings and other ritualistic methods, are also termed *mantra*. Hence, the word *mantra* is used in reference to various subjects.

3. Special Divisions
In this particular context, the topic of discussion concerns mantras that are recited. The divisions that were outlined above were merely general divisions of the categories that are referred to by the term *mantra*. In general, all vehicles of mantra are referred to as such because they afford protection efficiently and swiftly. The application of this term specifically to mantras that are recited is due to their status as extraordinary methods.

This variety of mantra is said to contain three general divisions: (1) secret mantra, (2) awareness mantra, and (3) retention mantra. In terms of the meaning they represent, the nature of these mantras can be correlated with emptiness, awareness, and unity, respectively. Alternatively, these three can also be applied in the reverse order. In terms of the symbolic form of the mudrā, the three types of mantra can be applied to the forms of two deities in union, a male deity, or a female deity, respectively. In terms of their own symbolism, it is also said that secret mantras are the form of the male deity, and the other two are the form of the female deity. Mantras can also be specifically correlated with the rituals taught in the traditions of unsurpassed mantra, outer mantra, and sūtra, respectively.

In terms of cause and function, mantras can be classified as follows. Extremely secret in essence, the wisdom of nondual method and knowledge manifesting as mantra serves to remedy misunderstanding. The identity of knowledge and wisdom manifesting in the form of mantra serves to remedy a lack of understanding. Finally, the nature of mindfulness and knowledge manifesting as mantra in the form of complete recall serves to remedy the degeneration of mindfulness. Even awareness mantras of male deities may have feminine suffixes since they dwell in the feminine deity of the basic space of emptiness. There are many such variations.

Alternatively, mantras can be classified as retention mantras in being blessed as mantras due to the attainment of the cause of retention; as awareness mantras in essentially being the embodiment of wisdom awareness; and secret mantras in being secret methods that are to be recited. Yet aside from classifying mantras based on conceptual distinctions, there is no essential difference between them. In such ways, various correlations can be made.

In particular, the mantras of any suitable maṇḍala involve the use of three types of mantra. First is the seed syllable, the root mantra that functions as the unerring cause. Second are the mantras that function as conditions for development, such as those that are recited during the development of a deity, the bestowal of empowerment, invocation, and offering. Third is the recitation of the activity mantra, the essence of the deity that is repeatedly recited. The latter category also possesses further subdivisions, such as the mantra of the primary deity, the mantras of the retinue, collective mantras, and supplementary activity mantras. Mantras can also be divided into those of approach, accomplishment, and activity; root mantras, essence mantras, and inner essence mantras; and in other ways. These various internal divisions are discussed in the tantras and practice manuals.

3. Accessing the Principle of Mantra
This section has three parts: (1) cultivating conviction in mantra with profound knowledge, (2) dwelling in the observation of mantra with profound absorption, and (3) perfecting the conduct of mantra with profound diligence.

1. Cultivating Conviction in Mantra with Profound Knowledge
This section has two parts: (1) viewing the deity and mantra as indivisible and (2) dispensing with the three notions that obstruct that view.

1. Viewing the Deity and Mantra as Indivisible
The principle of mantra should be ascertained via six designations. These are the same six that were discussed in the context of mudrā. Among these, one should gain conviction in the inseparability of the deity and mantra, which is the last of these six designations. Furthermore, one should perceive mantra itself to be the deity by realizing that (1) ultimately, all phenomena are undivided within the expanse of purity and equality, the great dharma body, and (2) relatively, there is no difference between the actual form of the deity and its mantra, insofar as both are merely manifestations of wisdom that manifest for the welfare of those in need of guidance.

2. Dispensing with the Three Notions That Obstruct That View
The first notion to dispense with is the idea that deity and mantra are truly different due to the qualities of their appearance. The wisdom of the buddhas can manifest in any way to those in need of guidance. As this is the case, they may appear as actual buddhas to guide some and as ordinary beings to guide others. There is, however, no difference between these two, insofar as both are the play of the wisdom of a single buddha. Hence, in truth, there is no qualitative difference. Similarly, here as well the Buddha manifests in the form of mantra to the perspective of ordinary beings. Meanwhile, even if the deity directly appears as a result of accomplishing mantra, what has been accomplished is the deity itself manifesting as mantra. Hence, the way in which the mantra itself manifests as the deity simply serves to bestow spiritual attainments upon those in need of guidance.

Second, one should dispense with the perception that deity and mantra are truly different because they have different forms. Some may get the idea that mantras are different from the deity because they have entirely different features. They may think that, being simply verbal expressions and letters written on a page, they lack any wisdom or other such qualities of their own.

If this were the case, however, the mind appearing in the form of material objects based on one's habitual tendencies, as when one is dreaming, and the Buddha's wisdom appearing as various enlightened bodies and pure realms, could not be subsumed under mind and wisdom, respectively. Moreover, when a single buddha manifests as the play of the infinite magical net with its peaceful and wrathful deities, then only one of those forms could be the deity, whereas the rest could not because they all have different features. In this way, it should be understood that, although deity and mantra appear in different forms, they are none other than the play of wisdom.

Third, one should dispense with the notion that deity and mantra are truly different because one appears in one's own being and the other appears in another's. According to this line of thinking, mantras and mudrās are part of one's own being, while the wisdom deity belongs to another's. Hence, these two are different. In response, it may be said that the deity of the definitive meaning is the natural state of all phenomena, the suchness of the ground of unity. This deity is the embodiment of self-occurring wisdom, the unified form that occurs once one is rid of all temporary impurities. Not realizing that this wisdom appears as the manifold magical net, if one were to think that a so-called "deity of another continuum" truly existed in a limited fashion with a body, speech, and mind in some isolated location, it would have component particles and instants of time. It would not, therefore, pervade all times and places or become the wisdom form in all its multiplicity. It would then necessarily follow that any deity seen anywhere other than the place where a deity dwells at a single point in time would not be the actual deity. However, we cannot say that of all the buddha forms that appear instantaneously in the sphere of perception of all the fortunate worldly beings in need of guidance, that one is the actual buddha and the rest are not. One must, therefore, train intelligently in the tradition of the great vehicle and understand that knowing the principle of buddhahood, at a bare minimum, is absolutely indispensable.

Having offered this general presentation, we will now bring the discussion back to the matter at hand. Mantras and other such factors may indeed appear to be part of one's own being. Nevertheless, in terms of their real being, the equality of reality itself, there are no established separate streams of being.

Moreover, this does not present any contradiction, even in terms of the way that things appear. What appears in one's own mind may in fact appear to be something "other," such as the appearances in a dream. On the other hand, groups of various disparate phenomena, such as the body, may appear to be a single phenomenon that is part of one's own being.

Though things appear in various ways, this is not how they actually are. Something may appear to be a part of one's own being or another's. Whatever the case, the appearance of mantra and mudrā carries out buddha activity and is able to gradually lead one to the state of buddhahood. Therefore, these appearances are held to be emanations of the wisdom of the bliss-gone ones. The way things appear to an ordinary mind cannot, on its own, negate the inconceivable experiential domains of the buddhas, who have attained mastery over all phenomena.

Furthermore, the blessings of the buddhas may appear in the experiential domains of dreams, states of absorption, and direct sense perception, yet in truth, they cannot be established as anything other than one's own self-display. The moment something appears to oneself, it is one's own self-display. As taught extensively in the scriptures, this can be established by reasoning based on the power of fact.

Therefore, according to the degree to which one's own mind has been divested of impurities, the miraculous displays and blessings of the buddhas will manifest more and more. In the end, these impurities will be completely purified and the way things actually are will manifest. Once this has come to pass, all the buddhas will be no different than oneself and one will be no different than all the buddhas. One will attain the body of wisdom, the intrinsic nature itself, a state of indivisibility with all the buddhas of the three times.

Hence, one should cultivate conviction that, at this point in time, the buddhas appear in the form of mantras to our perspective, and thereby accomplish both temporal and ultimate aims. Giving rise to this particular form of conviction in mantra is the primary cause for accomplishing it. Therefore, this principle is extremely important. The *Sādhana of the Single Hero Mañjuśrī* states:

> Through the way of secret mantras, the deity as such
> Will bestow all spiritual attainments.
> The practitioner of mantra who meditates on them,
> In accomplishing them, will gain accomplishment.

And in the *Request of Subāhu*:

> The one who knows of karma and its ripening
> Enters the forms of secret mantras
> In a way that agrees with all beings—
> To this guide of mantra I pay homage!

While the *Sambhūta* states:

> For the embodied, the form of mantra
> Enacts a great deal of activities.

And in the *Tantra of the Emergence of Cakrasaṃvara*:

> The mantra itself is the form of Yoginī
> And Yoginī herself is the form of the mantra.
> If one desires this exalted state,
> Do not separate these two.

Such quotes can be found in other scriptures as well.

2. Dwelling in the Observation of Mantra with Profound Absorption

This section has two parts: (1) the main part of practice—clear absorption and (2) the support—embracing the practice with the view.

1. The Main Part of Practice: Clear Absorption

In the main part of the practice, there are three principles: (1) clear appearance, (2) divine pride, and (3) the recollection of purity. First, the forms, spiritual life force, mantra chains, and radiation and absorption of light rays should be visualized with great clarity as the objects experienced in absorption. Second, without thinking of the deity as something that merely appears before the mind, one should have the divine pride of being indivisible from the deity. Third, the deity should not be viewed as something that exists as an individual stream of being, in a limited form with characteristics of its own name and form. Rather, one should recall that it is the ultimate fruitional wisdom, the perfection of abandonment and realization, that manifests in the form of the deity and mantra.

2. The Support: Embracing the Practice with the View

All of these factors never stray from the primordial state of the indivisible truths of purity and equality, the basic nature of the sole sphere of the dharma body. With this understanding, one should dwell with one-pointed concentration, uninterrupted by other forms of contemplation. Moreover, in the context of calm abiding, clarity, stability, and purity constitute insight into things in their multiplicity, while embracing this with the view constitutes insight into things as they are.

3. Perfecting the Conduct of Mantra with Profound Diligence

This section has three parts: (1) the preliminary steps, (2) the main part, and (3) the conclusion.

1. Preliminary

One who has received empowerment and abides by the samayas should please his or her guru and, by assembling mantras and so forth, correctly understand the key instructions concerning the purity of mantras and how to recite them.

2. Main Part

This section has three parts: (1) mental recitation, (2) whispered recitation, and (3) melodic recitation.

1. Mental Recitation

Mental mantra recitation does not involve any lip movement or other such effort. Rather, here the practitioner focuses on the mantra chain and seed syllable at the heart center and recites the mantra repeatedly in the mind, as if the mantra were naturally emitting its own sounds. There are two forms of mental recitation, simple mental recitation and mental recitation linked with the breath. The latter can itself be further divided into arrested recitation, vajra recitation, and vase breathing recitation.

The first of these is referred to as "arresting the life force and effort" and "restrained recitation." Here, "life force" refers to the energies, while "effort" refers to thoughts or the movements of mind. Thus, all energetic movements and effortful thoughts are inwardly restrained and recitation takes place in the mind. Through this, physical and verbal efforts are automatically blocked and extraordinary qualities are attained. With vajra recitation, the inhalation, exhalation, and resting of the breath are linked with mantra and one concentrates on the focal point without distraction. With vase breathing recitation, mantra recitation is joined with the fourfold vase breath and, again, recitation takes place in the mind.

2. Whispered Recitation

Though there is no melody in whispered recitation, sounds are whispered by applying a slight amount of effort to create motion in the lips and throat.

3. Melodic Recitation

There are six forms of melodic recitation. The first is a recitation that has ten qualities. The tone of the letters of the mantra should not be recited overly loud, soft, fast, or slow. They should be recited without speaking to others, while undistracted, without missing syllables, without extra syllables, with pure syllables that are free from any imperfections in the nasal ending and the other subtle elements of the mantra, and with clear pronunciation, meaning that the mantra is recited correctly and without distorting the source, function, and other aspects of each individual letter. The second is the tone of expelling the breath in the cheeks. Here, the tongue is placed on the palate, and the sound of the mantra is recited in a relaxed manner by expelling the breath through the nose as the air in the cheeks releases of its own accord, unperturbed and over an extended duration, producing a sound like the buzzing of bees. Third is the invocation of the melody of Brahma. In this approach, one recites the mantra in an enchanting manner, like the melody of Brahma. The voice is pleasing, subtle, and modulated, with the teeth clenched shut. Fourth is the melodic sound of groaning and lament. Here, the lips are closed and the tongue is placed on the palate. With a faint tone like an abandoned camel calf, here one recites as though one were groaning in lament. Fifth is the thunderous deep and resonant tone. With this approach, the tone is intense and forceful like thunder. The syllables are recited slightly fast and intensely, like water rushing off the face of a cliff. Sixth is the tone of the wail of the vajra demon. Here, the lips are closed and the mantra is recited like a bee caught in a jar, with unclear syllables and an intense tone like the cry of an angry demon.

These six are also referred to as the six melodies, which are known as *changka de'u*, *pangka de'u*, *dreng ngewa*, *tung ngewa*, *shartapa*, and *gartapa*, respectively. These melodies should be applied according to the context in which they are used. An alternative presentation lists the wail of the vajra demon as *shartapa*, the thunderous tone as *gartapa*, the recitation with one's breath in the cheeks as *changka de'u*, the tone of groaning in lament as *pangka de'u*, intoning the sound of mantra as *dreng ngewa*, and the melody of Brahma as *tung ngewa*. There are other presentations of the six tones as well.

When reciting mantra in these ways, one should maintain mindfulness and vigilance, avoiding any physical, verbal, or mental distractions. One should recite mantras in the correct manner, without losing sight of the view and meditation.

3. Conclusion

In between sessions, any adverse conditions that one encounters, such as being distracted by sense pleasures, should be avoided by understanding them to be obstacles. Moreover, one should not be discouraged if illness, negative forces, thoughts, or any other unfortunate circumstances develop. Rather, one should think that such occurrences are exhausting one's negative karma. Any factor that is taught to pose a threat to the accomplishment of mantra, such as keeping company of degenerates, should be cast far away. Things that are prohibited in other situations, such as meat and alcohol, are to be transformed into beneficial substances in secret mantra via mantra, visualization, and mudrā. One should, however, practice the various methods for gathering the accumulations and purifying obscurations, as these are conducive circumstances for the accomplishment of mantra. To purify one's being, one should have stable faith and firmly abide by the samayas and pledges one has made. One should also apply oneself to the instructions that develop the power of mantra, such as the recitation of the Sanskrit alphabet. Clothing, jewelry, food, drink, and all other such factors should be transformed into the play of wisdom by utilizing mantras, visualizations, and mudrās. In this way, adverse conditions should be avoided, while conducive circumstances should be assembled. Through this, the activity of accomplishing mantra should be brought to a point of culmination without letting up until mantra has been accomplished.

4. Purpose

Mantras function as the causes and conditions for emanating the deities of the maṇḍala. They are the principle of essential wisdom and the dharma seal. Through this, the deities are supremely pleased and the blessings of the buddhas enter one's being like brush catching fire, thereby incinerating the dense thicket of the obscurations and facilitating the emergence of retention, absorption, wisdom, and all the other qualities of the path. Mantras allow one to accomplish and attain the entire range of mundane and supreme spiritual attainments for the temporal and ultimate welfare of both oneself and others. Therefore, even a wish-fulfilling gem cannot illustrate mantra. Since mantras are themselves emanations of the buddhas, and since they carry out buddha activity and bring one to the state of buddhahood, they have a most sublime function.

In brief, what we refer to as *mantra* is the cause and essence of both deity and maṇḍala. It is what bestows empowerment, in addition to being a specific form of samaya. Mantra is the extraordinary gateway that employs seed syllables and other such principles to represent the view, and is the most sublime method to give rise to the profound view and meditation within one's own being. Mantra is the context of certain forms of meditation and conduct, the supreme method for sādhana practice and enlightened activity, and also that which seals the mudrā. Thus, mantra encompasses all aspects of training and, in those contexts, is the sole essential dharma. Moreover, since the essence of mantra is the wisdom deity, the view and all other such factors provide access to its nature.

In terms of their ultimate nature, mantras are equality, free of expressions and anything expressed. Hence, once all phenomena have reached a point of perfection within the expanse of the sole sphere of the dharma body, mantra will have reached a point of culmination and all the various forms of enlightened speech will be spontaneously present, without any need for intentional recitation. On this point, the *Tantra of the Secret Essence* states:

> The aspects of the maṇḍala of the singular enlightened speech
> Are inconceivable and all-pervasive.
> Resounding as individual sounds, names, and words,
> They are all the supreme seal of enlightened speech.

Concerning dwelling in reality itself, it is said that, "settling without speaking is the king of mantras."

Meanwhile, each and every verbalization is also mantra. The *Tantra of the Empowerment of Vajrapāṇi* states:

> While dwelling in a state of equality,
> Whatever movements of the limbs occur,
> Whatever words are verbalized,
> All are the mudrā of secret mantra.

This has been the section on the supreme method of mantra.

These last two sections conclude the clear explanation of the significance of mudrā and mantra, the perfection of method.

4. Conclusion: The Full and Complete Entrustment

This section has two parts: (1) entrusting the profound meaning of the tantra in a nondual manner and (2) the superiority of the recipients to whom this tantra is entrusted.

1. Entrusting the Profound Meaning of the Tantra in a Nondual Manner

Samantabhadra, Great Vajra Bliss, or Great Delight, is the teacher of this tantra. To his retinue of self-displayed wisdom, he called out this sincere advice:

> Hey! Hey! The nature or natural state of all phenomena throughout the ten directions and four times is primordially enlightened as great purity and equality. This nature, the very essence of the thus-gone ones, is known as the "secret essence," "great perfection," and by other such names. Though in truth we never stray from this primordial state of buddhahood, some do not realize this nature for what it is. In becoming obsessed with and fixated on their own dualistic constructs, they are held and bound by the noose of their very own thoughts. This is similar to seeing a white conch as yellow and other such examples. To avert this sort of delusion, the distinctions between the grounds and contexts of each individual vehicle are systematically presented. Although there are various such presentations, they are nothing more than paths leading to this ultimate vehicle of the secret essence. At the end of their

journey, buddhahood is achieved by entering this path. These vehicles, therefore, are steps along the path that leads here.

Hence, the buddhas possess the great wisdom that comes from perfecting the process of abandonment and realization. They have wondrous and infinite skillful methods for taming those in need of guidance, and there is nothing that they say that is not for the welfare of beings. On a temporal level, the various vehicles they teach each give rise to the abandonments and realizations of their respective paths, yet ultimately, they are methods that provide access to this secret essence.

Due to this principle, the most sacred seal of all the thus-gone ones throughout time and space is this great secret, the secret essence. Since there is no transcending it and it cannot be destroyed by anyone, this is the unique seal of buddhahood itself, like the seal that marks the command of a king. Hence, one who realizes this in the correct manner and imparts it flawlessly to another is no different from me, Samantabhadra. Empowerment as well will be naturally perfected. Therefore, be sure to uphold this text and do not let it disappear.

There are two ways to "uphold" the dharma: to practice the dharma of realization and to explain the dharma of scripture. Therefore, this tantra is upheld by realizing its meaning and then communicating it to others. This is the implicit entrustment. Once one has internalized this profound nature of reality, one will be indivisible with the wisdom mind of the teacher of this tantra. Empowerment will also be perfected since empowerment here means simply to give rise to this sort of profound wisdom.

For these reasons, if one turns one's back on the meaning of this secret essence—the primordial enlightenment of all that appears and exists—while doing such things as granting empowerments and explaining tantras, it will merely be a superficial charade. This is not what it means to uphold the tantra. It is even possible that those with inferior intellectual capacity will let this tantra go to waste, as stated in the *King Tantra of the Great Black One*:

> Senseless masters with no knowledge of the supremely profound
> will not even recall the words "nondual wisdom."

Therefore, when explaining the significance of great purity and equality, it is necessary to impart such teachings without departing from the way to elucidate according to the key instructions of the lineage of knowledge holders. Do not base your teachings on the discussions of childish, small-minded pedants, who only grasp certain terms that they readily understand.

Explaining the profound significance of this tantra incorrectly is an extremely grave mistake. The *Tantra of All-Embracing Awareness* states:

> Without the eye of dharma,
> Whatever boundless words one uses
> To express the conventions that convey meaning,
> One will be unable to discern whether it is correct or mistaken.
> Savage individuals who are concerned with words
> Are on the grounds and paths of training.
> However many hundreds of thousands of statements are made,
> They should not be taught to others.
> If taught, such thieves of the vajra teachings
> Will fall to Vajra Hell.
> If hypocrites who are not well versed
> In its meaning were to teach this dharma
> While remaining in ignorance themselves,
> They will have committed an act more serious
> Than murdering every sentient being.

This entrustment of the tantra was given in actuality to the self-displayed retinue and the Lord of Secrets. By implication, however, it was also entrusted through the power of intent to the mother deities and ḍākinīs who guard the samaya, and also to those individuals of the future who possess the eye of dharma.

There is also another way of explaining this, though in truth there is no difference between the two. In this approach, each couplet, beginning with the words, "Hey! Hey! . . . the ten directions and four times . . . ," is said to condense the entire meaning of the tantra into four types of appearance. Respectively, these four provide instructions on (1) the natural appearances of the ground (which are to be realized), (2) the deluded perceptions of misguided beliefs (which are to be purified), (3) the appearances of the path by those in need of guidance (which are to be traversed), and (4) the fruitional appearances of the bliss-gone ones (which are to be attained). Hence, the tantra is held to have been entrusted to the retinue by providing instructions on these four types of appearance.

2. The Superiority of the Recipients to Whom This Tantra Is Entrusted

What all the thus-gone ones of the ten directions master is none other than this ultimate secret of the enlightened body, speech, and mind. Thus, in being designated as the wisdom of the noble ones, it is the ultimate definitive meaning. In teaching the meaning of the natural state as it is, the entire range of extreme exaggerations and denigrations are thoroughly pacified. This reality, the secret essence, is perfect, supreme, and sublime.

This is the secret essence insofar as this nature emerged from the basic space of the definitive mind of Samantabhadra and was then taught to the retinue or, alternately, because it is the profound secret of the victorious ones. That which emerges from the expanse of Samantabhadra's enlightened mind, the basic space where reality is ascertained and where exaggerations and denigrations have been pacified, is the individual that realizes the meaning of this tantra. This is so because, in the way that waves well up from the ocean, the self-expression of wisdom appearances emerge from the basic space of the ground, which is inseparable from the realization of all the victorious ones of the three times. Hence, individuals who correctly realize their own natural state are none other than this state.

Such an individual will be confirmed by glorious Samantabhadra, the teacher of this tantra, who will grant a prophecy that he or she will not return and will swiftly attain buddhahood. Like the eldest son of a universal emperor becoming crown prince, such an individual will be the sacred offspring of the bliss-gone ones. Hence, they are said to be "born from the enlightened mind of all the buddhas" since they arise from this secret of the enlightened mind.

Therefore, those who impart this tantra to others are beings of awareness, and they will be prophesied to dwell upon the supreme and most sublime of all grounds, the so-called "ground of the knowledge holder," "the ground of the vajra holder," "the ground of supreme method and knowledge," "the thirteenth ground of buddhahood," and "the ultimate ground." Said differently, when a beggar is trying to find a treasure of jewels that is buried beneath his home, those who have yet to see the treasure may indeed refer to him as a beggar. Nevertheless, he is also rich, in the sense of having definitively established himself as the owner of the precious treasure. Likewise, this is also likened to having hooked a fish but not yet landed it. Though it may still be in the water, it is similar to having it on dry land. Just so, here one is said to dwell on the ground of perfection.

In brief, the most sublime of all the contexts, or grounds, of the lower vehicles is the ground of this ultimate mantra vehicle, for this is the realization of self-occurring wisdom—the naturally luminous maṇḍala of mind. In other words, it is the realization of the reality of mantra that sets this ground apart. With this realization, one can be called a "knowledge holder," a "vajra holder," and a "mantra wielder." By merely freeing oneself from doubt and gaining certainty concerning the reality of mantra, one will be prophesied to become a nonreturner. If it can be said that merely seeing the symbolic illustrative maṇḍala brings the benefit of not returning and attaining buddhahood, why even mention that this will be the case if one realizes the true maṇḍala that is illustrated, the reality of mantra—indivisible purity and equality.

Here, what we refer to as "realization" is the certainty that comes about once a beginner has used the faculty of knowledge to cut through superimpositions. Therefore, beginners who have entered the ground of mantra in the correct manner, no matter how lowly, are destined for enlightenment, equal in fortune to a nonreturning bodhisattva. Moreover, since their paths are even swifter than the bodhisattvas, their destinies are even equal to those in their last existence, and so on.

Here, in saying "entered in the correct manner," what is meant is that one has received empowerment and gained conviction in the wisdom of the empowerment's nature—the great purity and equality of all that appears and exists. Hence, one must strive to gain conviction in the reality of mantra. As stated in the *Vajra Mirror*:

> To reveal the tantra of the wisdom of self-awareness
> It is manifested through the awareness of self-display—
> This is the supreme knowledge holder.
> Yet even without the power of spontaneously present absorption,
> One is unswayed by bodhisattvas training on the grounds,
> For one's experiential domain is the same as the bliss-gone ones'.
> They will receive the confirmation of an awareness being.

In the *Sūtra That Gathers All Intents*, it is said:

> To elucidate the secret enlightened mind
> Of the victorious ones, having realized it oneself,
> Is the most supreme of all empowerments—
> The empowerment of the three worlds.

And:

> The blessings and qualities that come from realizing the essential meaning
> For just an instant cannot be fully expressed by the victorious ones.
> Ultimate goodness and all merit
> Can be likened to the dust on a fingernail,
> While generating the vajra essence just once
> Is equal to a vast maṇḍala of earth.

For these reasons, the knowledge holders are unrivaled throughout the world as objects of veneration. Again, the *Sūtra That Gathers All Intents* explains:

> To such a sacred meaningful being,
> Throughout all of the three times,
> All of the victorious bliss-gone ones
> From all the realms in the ten directions
> Come, paying homage with praises and interest.

And:

> Even if those who hold the secret vajra essence
> Were to engage in no activities other than
> Mounting a chariot, a horse, or otherwise,
> The victors would honor their mount with the crowns of their heads.

And in the *Subsequent Tantra of the Secret Gathering*:

> Whoever sees or touches one who has accomplished the main deity,
> Clearly remembers him or simply hears his name,

Shows faith or only does one of these,
Will view that person as vajra enlightenment and always pay homage.

Furthermore, the beneficial qualities that come from merely becoming interested in the approach of secret mantra are limitless. The *Sūtra That Gathers All Intents* states:

Though one may lack the strength of knowing the essential meaning,
Merely generating this intention will outshine the Middle Way.

And:

For those who are attracted to and become interested in
This secret of the victorious ones,
Others will not create obstacles
And they will swiftly attain what they desire.

Other such quotes are found extensively throughout the tantras.

This concludes the general overview of the text, in which the points covered in the subject matter of the tantra were condensed into the three continua and eleven principles.

3. Extensive Explanation of the Meaning Expressed through the Words of the Tantra

For a more extensive presentation of the expressions employed by the tantra, one may consult the clear explanations of Rongzom and Longchenpa. This overview of the great king of tantras, using study and contemplation to eliminate superimpositions concerning the approach of the path of the unsurpassed mantra, provides access to this approach. These few vital points, moreover, were given in a condensed manner according to the general lineage of the knowledge holders, but especially according to the enlightened viewpoints of the Omniscient Lord of Dharma and glorious Rongzom Mahāpaṇḍita. Nevertheless, experiencing these profound vital points nakedly in one's own being depends on whether or not one has encountered a qualified master with experience of the key instructions of the lineage of knowledge holders and the lineage of blessings. From such a master, one must be ripened through empowerment, receive the blessings of the true lineage, and listen to the profound and liberating key instructions directly from his or her mouth.

The meaning that is taught in the precious tantra section of the Nyingma's mantra tradition is contained in these profound key points on mantra that are transmitted orally from the mouths of the knowledge holders. In other traditions, these points are not fully expressed. Candrakīrti similarly states:

> Aside from this, elsewhere this dharma
> Is not genuinely found.
> Similarly, elsewhere, the tradition that originates here is absent.
> O learned ones, of this be sure.

Therefore, keeping in mind how rare they are, these teachings should be treasured and maintained. It is inappropriate to offer them wantonly to the faithless and narrow minded. The celestial ḍākinīs, moreover, are said to safeguard teachings like this on the profound meaning of mantra as though they were the essential blood flowing through their hearts. Hence, it should be kept secret from those who are not fit to receive such teachings. Wise, fortunate individuals, on the other hand, those with great faith in mantra, should be taught well, thereby ensuring that these precious essential teachings on the secret mantra spread throughout all space and time.

> Though in terms of time and place we are inferior people,
> Through the unpolluted ocean of faith in our hearts,
> The moon and stars of the blessings of the lineage of knowledge
>   holders,
> Will, I feel, be instantly reflected in our minds.

> The benevolent master, the primordial protector,
> Offered words of sanction, time and time again.
> Through the force of being entrusted with the intent of his joyful
>   mind
> I gained slight confidence to say something about this approach.

> Whatever faults there may be in having nakedly revealed this
>   profound secret,

And any faults arising from my own mind, I confess to the deities
 of the three roots.
Through the virtue of offering this clear explanation based on the key
 instructions
Of the master and the scriptures of the lineage of knowledge holders,

May pure appearances equal to the basic space of phenomena,
Supremely luminous and blissful in essence,
Through the state of nectar, gentle and glorious,
Bestow sublime joy upon the minds of all beings!

With the victory banner of the teachings of the fearless ancient
 translations held aloft,
And the royal drum of the dharmas of scripture and realization
 resounding in all directions,
May the lion's roar of the tradition of reason pervade the three worlds,
And may the light of unparalleled virtuous omens flourish!

From Pema Ösel Do-ngak Lingpa, the great fearless master and regent of the victorious lord Padmasambhava, I received numerous encouragements to compose this text. In particular, at the time of offering a feast in conjunction with the anniversary of the Great Omniscient One, I requested permission to write this from the deities of the three roots and was then given permission with the words, "Begin this very day!"

On this basis, I, Jampal Gyeypé Dorjé, offered ten thousand butter lamps, a feast offering, and so forth, then prayed fervently to the assembly of deities of the three roots. I then set out to compose the text with the intelligence of remaining in the light of the scriptures of the lineage of knowledge holders and the enlightened speech of the masters, the glorious protectors. I completed the composition on the sacred tenth day of the third month in the year of the Earth Protector. Through this, may the essential teachings of secret mantra spread and flourish throughout all space and time, and may this cause all beings to attain the state of supreme enlightenment! Virtue! Virtue! Virtue!

APPENDIX A:
Topical Outline of *Luminous Essence*

1) The Magnificence of the Tantra
2) The Meaning of the Tantra
    1) The Title
    2) A Summary of the Essential Points of the Meaning of the Text's Subject Matter
        1) The Purpose and Relevance of the Tantra
        2) Presenting the Meaning of the Tantra
            (1) The Setting
            (2) The Prelude
            (3) The Meaning of the Tantra
                (1) A General Presentation of the Principles of the Three Continua
                    (1) The Ground Continuum
                        1. The Natural Maṇḍala of the Ground
                        2. How Delusion Arises
                        3. Delusion and the Natural Ground
                        4. The Reversal of Delusion
                    (2) The Path Continuum
                        1. The Essence of the Path
                        2. The Divisions of the Path
                            1. A General Explanation
                                1. The Two Vehicles
                                2. The Five Vehicles
                                3. The Nine Vehicles
                            2. The Path of Unsurpassable Mantra
                                1. Development and Completion
                                2. Means and Liberation
                        3. Traversing the Path

            (3) The Fruition Continuum
        (2) Specific Explanation of the Path Continuum
            (1) Various Classification Schemes
            (2) The Present Context
                1. View
                2. Absorption
                3. Conduct
                4. Maṇḍala
                5. Empowerment
                6. Samayas
                7. Accomplishment
                8. Offerings
                9. Enlightened Activity
                10. Mudrā
                11. Mantra
        (4) Conclusion: The Full and Complete Entrustment
            (1) Entrusting the Profound Meaning of the Tantra in a Nondual Manner
            (2) The Superiority of the Recipients to Whom This Tantra Is Entrusted
    3) Extensive Explanation of the Meaning Expressed through the Words of the Tantra

APPENDIX B:
Expanded Outline of the Topic "The Present Context" from the Topical Outline of *Luminous Essence*

1) View
    1) Essence
        (1) The Common, General Explanation
        (2) The Extraordinary, Specific Explanation
    2) Divisions
    3) Establishing the View through Reasoning
        (1) The Superiority of the Mantric View
        (2) The View of Mantra
            (1) Individual Elements of the View
                (1) Purity
                    1. The Principle of Purity
                        1. The Divinity of Appearances
                            1. Conventional Valid Cognition
                            2. Purity and Ultimate Valid Cognition
                        2. The Subject as Wisdom
                    2. Relinquishing the Untenability of Purity
                (2) Equality
                    1. Arguments for Equality
                    2. Gaining Certainty about Equality
                (3) Inseparability
            (2) General Explanations
                (1) Directly Establishing the Meaning
                (2) Indirectly Establishing the Meaning
    4) Purpose
        (1) General Purpose
        (2) Specific Purpose

2) **Absorption**
    1) Essence
    2) Divisions
        (1) Essential Divisions
        (2) Temporal Divisions
    3) The Practice of Meditative Absorption
    4) Purpose

3) **Conduct**
    1) Essence
    2) Divisions
    3) Principles
    4) Purpose

4) **Maṇḍala**
    1) Essence
    2) Divisions
    3) Principle
    4) Purpose

5) **Empowerment**
    1) Essence
    2) Divisions
    3) Principle
    4) Purpose

6) **Samayas**
    1) Essence
    2) Divisions
        (1) General Divisions
        (2) Specific Divisions
        (3) The Five Root Samayas
            (1) Not Discarding the Unsurpassable
            (2) Respecting the Master
            (3) Not Interrupting the Continuity of Mantra and Mudrā
            (4) Loving Those Who Have Entered the Authentic Path
            (5) Not Explaining the Secret Meaning to Unqualified Recipients
        (4) The Ten Subsidiary Samayas
            (1) Not Abandoning the Five Poisons

           (1) Disturbing Emotions and the Buddha Families
           (2) Taking Disturbing Emotions as the Path
           (3) Disturbing Emotions as the Essence of Wisdom
       (2) Not Discarding the Five Nectars
   3) The Principles of the Key Points of Samaya
   4) Purpose
       (1) The General Purpose
       (2) The Specific Purpose

7) **Accomplishment**
   1) Essence
   2) Divisions
       (1) General Explanation
       (2) Group Accomplishment
   3) Principle
       (1) How to Achieve Accomplishment
       (2) The Fruition of Accomplishment
   4) Purpose

8) **Offerings**
   1) Essence
   2) Divisions
       (1) The Unique Specific Divisions
       (2) The Common Gathering Circle
   3) Principle
   4) Purpose

9) **Enlightened Activity**
   1) Essence
   2) Divisions
   3) Principle
   4) Purpose

10) **Mudrā**
    1) Essence
    2) Divisions
        (1) General Presentation
        (2) Specific Presentation
            (1) Seals in the Development Stage

        (2) Seals in the Completion Stage
    (3) Special Presentation
  3) Principle
    (1) Understanding the Principle of the Seals
    (2) Understanding How Mudrās Are Used to Seal
  4) Purpose

11) **Mantra**
  1) Essence
    (1) Letters: The Cause of Mantras
    (2) The Four Establishments: The Essence of Mantra
    (3) Unimpeded Ability: The Effect of Mantra
  2) Divisions
    (1) General Divisions
    (2) Specific Divisions
    (3) Special Divisions
  3) Accessing the Principle of Mantra
    (1) Cultivating Conviction in Mantra with Profound Knowledge
      (1) Viewing the Deity and Mantra as Indivisible
      (2) Dispensing with the Three Notions That Obstruct That View
    (2) Dwelling in the Observation of Mantra with Profound Absorption
      (1) The Main Part of Practice: Clear Absorption
      (2) The Support: Embracing the Practice with the View
    (3) Perfecting the Conduct of Mantra with Profound Diligence
      (1) Preliminary
      (2) Main Part
        (1) Mental Recitation
        (2) Whispered Recitation
        (3) Melodic Recitation
      (3) Conclusion
  4) Purpose

APPENDIX C:
Visual Outline of *Luminous Essence*

Please see next page

Luminous Essence

1. The Magnificence of the Tantra

2. The Meaning of the Tantra

1. The Title

2. A Summary of the Essential Points of the Meaning of the Text's Subject Matter

1. The Purpose and Relevance of the Tantra

2. Presenting the Meaning of the Tantra

1. The Setting
2. The Prelude
3. The Meaning of the Tantra

1. A General Presentation of the Principles of the Three Continua

####### 1. The Ground Continuum
1. The Natural Maṇḍala of the Ground
2. How Delusion Arises
3. Delusion and the Natural Ground
4. The Reversal of Delusion

####### 1. The Path Continuum
1. The Essence of the Path
2. The Divisions of the Path
   1. A General Explanation
      1. The Two Vehicles
      2. The Five Vehicles
      3. The Nine Vehicles
   2. The Path of Unsurpassable Mantra
      1. Development and Completion
      2. Means and Liberation
3. Traversing the Path

####### 1. The Fruition Continuum

2. Specific Explanation of the Path Continuum

See next double page…

4. Conclusion: The Full and Complete Entrustment
1. Entrusting the Profound Meaning of the Tantra in a Nondual Manner
2. The Superiority of the Recipients to Whom This Tantra Is Entrusted

3. Extensive Explanation of the Meaning Expressed through the Words of the Tantra

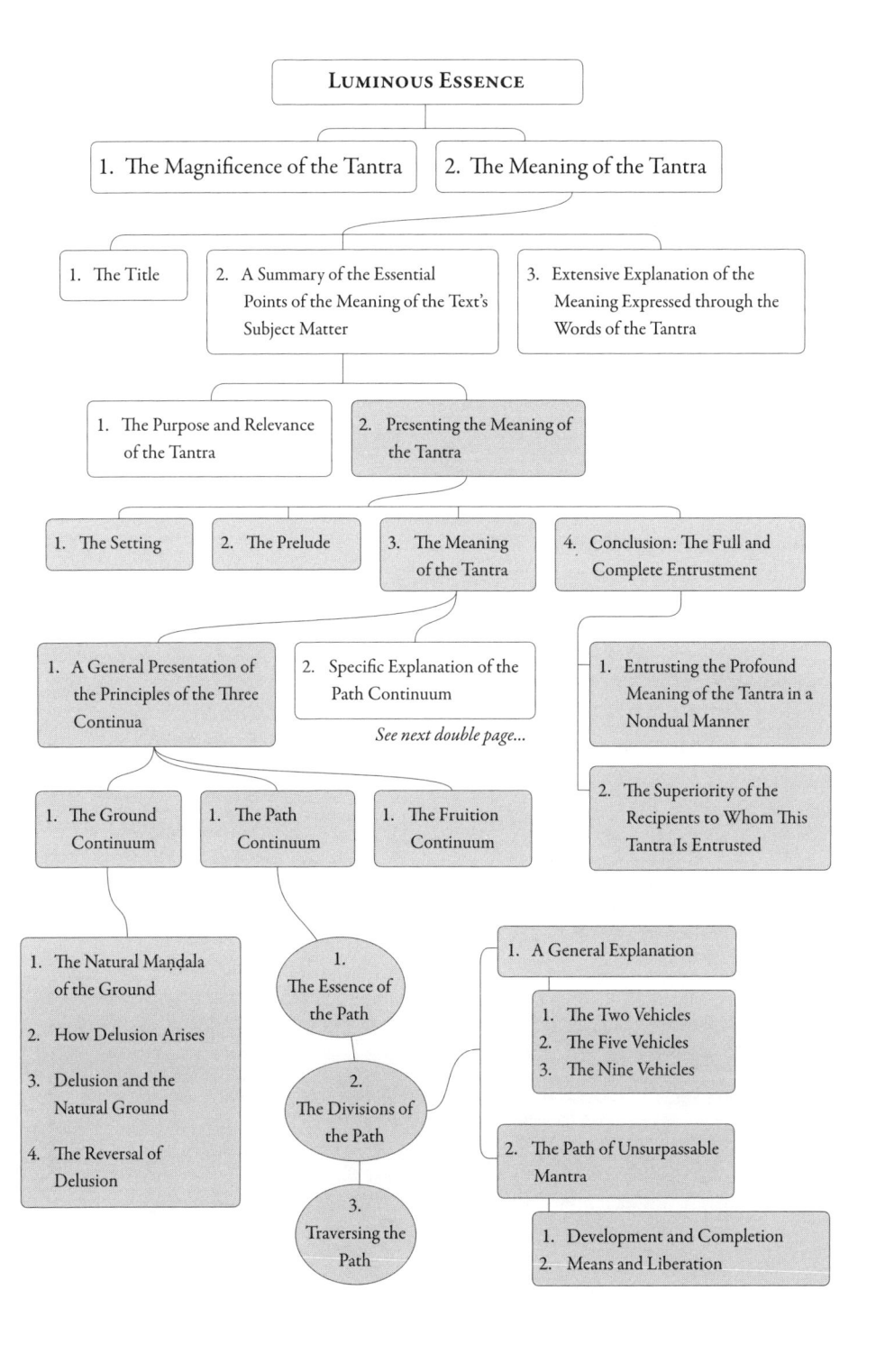

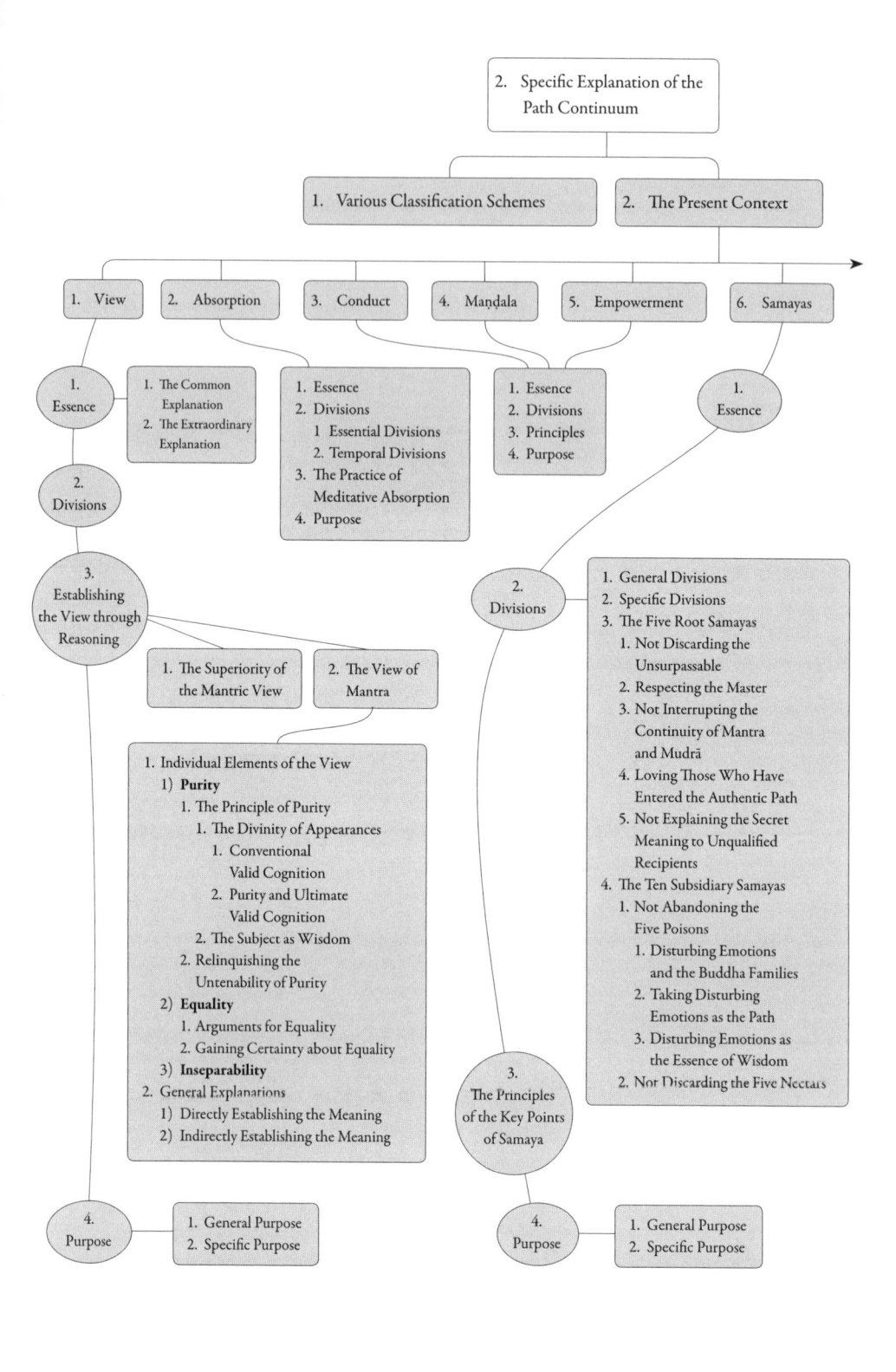

2. Specific Explanation of the Path Continuum

- 1. Various Classification Schemes
- 2. The Present Context
  - 1. View
    - 1. Essence
    - 2. Divisions
    - 3. Establishing the View through Reasoning
      - 1. The Superiority of the Mantric View
      - 2. The View of Mantra
        - 1. Individual Elements of the View
          - 1) **Purity**
            - 1. The Principle of Purity
              - 1. The Divinity of Appearances
                - 1. Conventional Valid Cognition
                - 2. Purity and Ultimate Valid Cognition
              - 2. The Subject as Wisdom
            - 2. Relinquishing the Untenability of Purity
          - 2) **Equality**
            - 1. Arguments for Equality
            - 2. Gaining Certainty about Equality
          - 3) **Inseparability**
        - 2. General Explanations
          - 1) Directly Establishing the Meaning
          - 2) Indirectly Establishing the Meaning
    - 4. Purpose
      - 1. General Purpose
      - 2. Specific Purpose
  - 2. Absorption
    - 1. The Common Explanation
    - 2. The Extraordinary Explanation
  - 3. Conduct
    - 1. Essence
    - 2. Divisions
      - 1 Essential Divisions
      - 2. Temporal Divisions
    - 3. The Practice of Meditative Absorption
    - 4. Purpose
  - 4. Maṇḍala
  - 5. Empowerment
    - 1. Essence
    - 2. Divisions
    - 3. Principles
    - 4. Purpose
  - 6. Samayas
    - 1. Essence
    - 2. Divisions
      - 1. General Divisions
      - 2. Specific Divisions
      - 3. The Five Root Samayas
        - 1. Not Discarding the Unsurpassable
        - 2. Respecting the Master
        - 3. Not Interrupting the Continuity of Mantra and Mudrā
        - 4. Loving Those Who Have Entered the Authentic Path
        - 5. Not Explaining the Secret Meaning to Unqualified Recipients
      - 4. The Ten Subsidiary Samayas
        - 1. Not Abandoning the Five Poisons
          - 1. Disturbing Emotions and the Buddha Families
          - 2. Taking Disturbing Emotions as the Path
          - 3. Disturbing Emotions as the Essence of Wisdom
        - 2. Not Discarding the Five Nectars
    - 3. The Principles of the Key Points of Samaya
    - 4. Purpose
      - 1. General Purpose
      - 2. Specific Purpose

7. Accomplishment

1. Essence
2. Divisions
   1. General Explanation
   2. Group Accomplishment
3. Principle
   1. How to Achieve Accomplishment
   2. The Fruition of Accomplishment
4. Purpose

8. Offerings

1. Essence
2. Divisions
   1. The Unique Specific Divisions
   2. The Common Gathering Circle
3. Principle
4. Purpose

9. Enlightened Activity

1. Essence
2. Divisions
3. Principle
4. Purpose

10. Mudrā

1. Essence
2. Divisions
   1. General Presentation
   2. Specific Presentation
      1. Seals in the Development Stage
      2. Seals in the Completion Stage
   3. Special Presentation
3. Principle
   1. Understanding the Principle of the Seals
   2. Understanding How Mudrās Are Used to Seal
4. Purpose

11. Mantra

1. Essence
   1. Letters: The Cause of Mantras
   2. The Four Establishments: The Essence of Mantra
   3. Unimpeded Ability: The Effect of Mantra
2. Divisions
   1. General Divisions
   2. Specific Divisions
   3. Special Divisions
3. Accessing the Principle of Mantra
   1. Cultivating Conviction in Mantra with Profound Knowledge
      1. Viewing the Deity and Mantra as Indivisible
      2. Dispensing with the Three Notions That Obstruct That View
   2. Dwelling in the Observation of Mantra with Profound Absorption
      1. The Main Part of Practice: Clear Absorption
      2. The Support: Embracing the Practice with the View
   3. Perfecting the Conduct of Mantra with Profound Diligence
      1. Preliminary
      2. Main Part
         1. Mental Recitation
         2. Whispered Recitation
         3. Melodic Recitation
      3. Conclusion
4. Purpose

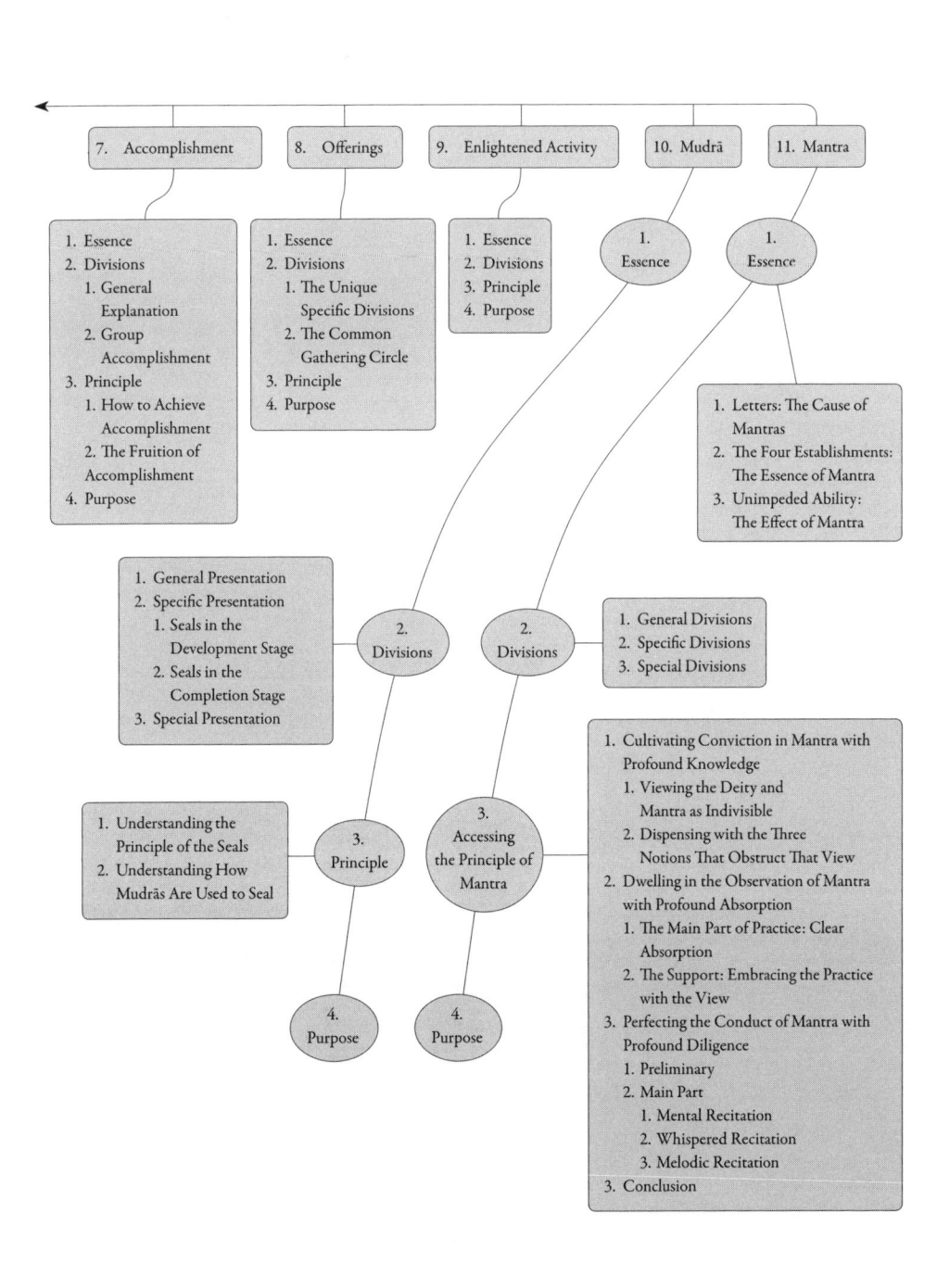